I forgot to buy you a birthday present! (Ages ago though it was)

Beyond
ASLAN

ESSAYS ON C.S. LEWIS

EDITED BY BURTON K. JANES

God bless

Love

chris

XXX

Bridge-Logos
Gainesville, Florida

Bridge-Logos

Gainesville, FL 32614 USA

Beyond Aslan: Essays on C.S. Lewis
Edited by Burton K. Janes

Printed in the United States of America.

Library of Congress Catalog Card Number: 2005936840
International Standard Book Number 0-88270-082-0

Photo Credits:
Cover photo used by permission of The Marion E. Wade Center, Wheaton College, Wheaton, IL.

Dedicated to the memory of
Stephen L. Schofield (1915-93),
the founding publisher and editor of
The Canadian C.S. Lewis Journal.

Don't say in grief he is no more
But rather in thankfulness that he was.

–An old Hebrew proverb

ABOUT THE MASTHEAD YOU SEE
"ENGRAVED" INTO THE COVER

The Masthead, which first appeared in issue #88 of *The Canadian C.S. Lewis Journal*, is a gift from Pauline Baynes. After she illustrated J.R.R. Tolkien's *Farmer Giles of Ham*, C.S. Lewis selected her to illustrate his Chronicles of Narnia. Pauline explains the symbolism of her design as follows: "I have depicted Aslan, of course, books, pen and ink, the famous Lewis pipes and beer stein, plus maple leaf and English rose, Magdalen College, the devil (from *Screwtape*, and in whom Lewis believed), Europa on the bull (= the Greek mythological background), courtly love and a knight (his love of Medieval poetry), the Irish shamrock, and some of the Narnian characters: the lamppost, Reepicheep, Puddleglum and Mr. Tumnus."

TABLE OF CONTENTS

Foreword by Rev. Perry C. Bramlett   page xi

Introduction   page xv

Beyond Aslan Album   page xix

Lewisiana

C.S. Lewis: Mere Christian   page 1
by Roger J. Stronstad

C.S. Lewis and Weather   page 7
by the late Evan K. Gibson

Humour and Spirituality: Cheerful Givers   page 11
by Darin Harootunian

The Screwtape Letters: Of Greed and Grace   page 17
by Jack L. Knowles

C.S. Lewis and the Holy Spirit   page 29
by the late Kathryn Lindskoog

Frightened by Unicorns: page 35
The Narrator of *The Great Divorce*
by George Musacchio

Trained Habit: The Spirituality of C.S. Lewis   page 41
by Nancy-Lou Patterson

Assessing the Apologetics of C.S. Lewis   page 59
by Clark H. Pinnock

C.S. Lewis as the Patron Saint   page 69
of American Evangelicalism
by Philip Graham Ryken

Death and Dying in the Writings of C.S. Lewis   page 83
     by Peter J. Schakel

Touchstone of Reality: Great Awakenings   page 99
     by Micahel A. Szuk

The Agony and the Ecstasy of C.S. Lewis   page 105
     by Walter Unger

Visiting C.S. Lewis's Oxford   page 115
     by Diane Vint

Testimonials

How I Became Interested in C.S. Lewis   page 121
     by Carolyn Keefe

From G.K. Chesterton to C.S. Lewis   page 127
     by Peter Milward, S.J.

Narnia

The Lion, the Witch, and the Wastebasket: page 135
     Discarded Fragments of the Narnia Chronicles
     by David C. Downing

To Narnia and Back   page 147
     by Martha A. Emmert

The Lion, the Witch and the Wardrobe: page 153
     Through Eight-Year-Old Eyes
     Collected by Roger J. Stronstad

The Lion, the Witch and the Wardrobe at 50:   page 157
     A Celebration (and a Worry)
     by Paul F. Ford

Family Connections

Helen Joy Lewis   page 179
    by *Douglas Gresham*

W.H. Lewis: Popular Historian   page 185
    by *Charles J. Wrong*

Sightings

"An Examiner's Nightmare" / "Awake, My Lute!"   page 195
    by *Burton K. Janes*

Bob Jones, Jr. Meets C.S. Lewis   page 201
    by *Burton K. Janes*

C.S. Lewis's Honourary Degrees   page 205
    by *Burton K. Janes*

A Little-Known C.S. Lewis Letter   page 213
    by *Burton K. Janes*

Sherwood Eliot Wirt Interviews C.S. Lewis   page 219
    by *Burton K. Janes*

Appendix

Stephen L. Schofield (1915-93)   page 225
    by *Burton K. Janes*

FOREWORD

It was a pleasure to be asked to write a foreword for this book, which is the third published collection of articles and essays to come from *The Canadian C.S. Lewis Journal*. The first, published in 1983 (has it been that long?), was called *In Search of C.S. Lewis* and was edited by the late and sorely missed Stephen Schofield. That work, while well-balanced and containing many stimulating and informative articles about and concerning Lewis, did not sell quite as well as it should have and thus was largely unknown to the popular reading public. I fervently hope that this present volume will be read by everyone who loves and cares about C.S. Lewis and who wants to know more about him.

The Canadian C.S. Lewis Journal has played a significant role in my life and what I do as a vocation. In the late 1970s I was living in Birmingham, Alabama, working for a well-known national magazine and preparing to get married and enter a theological seminary. One summer day I was visiting a local antique store, something I love to do even to this day as a way to relax. I looked at and eventually bought (for 25 cents) a copy of a journal. I recognized the face on the cover, because I had started reading C.S. Lewis's books, staring with *The Screwtape Letters*, about ten years earlier. I did not notice it right away, but the journal I bought that day was the first issue of *The Canadian C.S. Lewis Journal*, published in January 1979. How it ended up in an antique store in the deep south I will never know, for there was no subscription sticker on it.

I was very naive about Lewis at that time, and had read very little *about* him. But in this issue, one article in particular caught and sustained my attention. It was titled "Exhilaration," and was an interview by Mr. Schofield of Lewis's former student, the drama critic and theatrical producer Kenneth Tynan. I was immediately enthralled. Mr. Tyman talked about Lewis in ways and in obvious admiration that thrilled me and held my attention and left me wanting more. He told of Lewis's prodigious memory, his great literary gifts, his unpretentiousness, and finally his encouraging personal comments. I was, as many people say about Lewis, hooked. As I read further and deeper in the issue, I noticed also that on the last page, Mr. Schofield mentioned that later issues of *The Canadian C.S. Lewis Journal* would answer questions about Lewis, such as why he was never made a professor at Oxford, why he married a dying divorcee, why he went to Cambridge, and others. I immediately wrote and ordered a years' worth of twelve issues (for seven dollars); if I remember correctly I received only six. But that did not matter. I was not only now hooked on what Lewis wrote, I was hooked on what had been and was being written about him.

About nine or so years later, I was living in Louisville, Kentucky, married, a seminary graduate, and wondering what to do. I was thinking (and agonizing) about starting a speaking, teaching and writing ministry about Lewis, and had no earthly (or heavenly) idea of what to do or how to go about it. I looked in my library and saw one of my favourite books, *C.S. Lewis: Mere Christian*, by someone named Kathryn Lindskoog. I knew nothing about Lindskoog, except that her writing seemed "friendly" and intelligent, that she had written often about Lewis, and most importantly, that she had met him and *he* valued her work. What a compliment! So I called her in California and told her who I was and what I wanted to do, and asked her a slew of somewhat (I realized later) anxious questions. She first told me to call her "Kay," then she very patiently and warmly answered all my questions, even (as I surmised later) the most obvious ones. Kay told me to indeed take Lewis to the churches, because "the academics have Lewis and know him already; it's the regular people in the pews who need and want him the most." When I asked her what were the best reference books on Lewis, she mentioned a few; I remember the Hooper/Green first biography (1974) and Dr. Clyde Kilby's wonderful pictorial biography, *C.S. Lewis: Images of His World*. Then Kay said, "But before you read these, read the journals if you aren't doing that already. You can start with *The Canadian C.S. Lewis Journal*." When I told her I knew about and had read that one already, she said, "Good. Most of the stuff in it is well-written, and it's persnickity and uneven in format, and isn't perfect, but it's fun, and it will whet your appetite for more and more of Lewis."

Kay Lindskoog and I became good friends, and she became, in one sense, my "Lewis mentor." I found out later that she knew Mr. Schofield and had written for *The Canadian C.S. Lewis Journal*. Without her encouragement, and that also from other good friends and family, I might not have started a ministry that is now at the end of its seventeenth year. Kay was right about *The Canadian C.S. Lewis Journal*. It did whet my appetite for more and more of Lewis, and I did eventually obtain every issue, and now I read them (again) periodically. When I speak at churches I carry that over and tell folks that all I can really do for them in a short period of time is to whet their their appetites for Lewis and ask them to seriously consider what he wrote and how he lived as a "mere Christian." I also tell them that Lewis could at times be persnickity, and that he was always interesting and fun. Often the folks at churches listen to me, and sometimes they ask me what to read *about* Lewis. When I mention books, especially by well-known authors, they listen and even occasionally tell me later that they bought so and so. When I mention journals and newsletters, and offer to give them addresses where they can order back issues of *The Canadian C.S. Lewis Journal* and others, most of them do not accept my offer, but some do.

The C.S. Lewis journals available now are often very good and informative and I get them all eventually, but they are not quite the same for me as was, and still is, *The Canadian C.S. Lewis Journal*. Sadly, it is no longer published, but thanks to the talented Rev. Burton Janes and a cast of very good writers (including Kay Lindskoog), essays and articles from this persnickity and highly entertaining publication are available once again. I am quite confident that what you will read and savour in this book will indeed whet your appetite for more and more of C.S. Lewis, like an old twenty-five-cent journal did for me years ago. And I do not know what will happen to you, but I haven't been the same since ...

Rev. Perry C. Bramlett
C.S. *Lewis for the Local Church - Interstate Ministries*
Louisville, Kentucky

REV. PERRY C. BRAMLETT

Rev. Perry C. Bramlett is the founder of "C.S. Lewis for the Local Church - Interstate Ministries," a nationwide speaking ministry on the life, works and influence of Lewis. The ministry is now at the end of its seventeenth year.

Perry is the only person in the United States who teaches and writes about C.S. Lewis and J.R.R. Tolkien as a full-time vocation. He has given nearly 2,000 hours of talks and retreats to churches, colleges and groups in twenty-five states on Lewis, Tolkien, their friends and influences, and other great Christian storytellers. He has been quoted in many newspapers and magazines, including *The Christian Science Monitor* and the *Louisville Courier-Journal*.

Perry's books include *C.S. Lewis: Life at the Centre* (Peake Road, an imprint of Smyth and Helwys Publishing, 1996); *I Am in Fact a Hobbit: An Introduction to the Life and Work of J.R.R. Tolkien* (Mercer University Press, 2003); with Ronald W. Higdon, *Touring C.S. Lewis' Ireland and England: A travel guide to C.S. Lewis' favourite places to walk and visit* (Smyth and Helwys Publishing, 1998); and *A C.S. Lewis Spiritual Reader* (forthcoming).

He has written articles, reviews and sermons for *Preaching, The Canadian C.S. Lewis Journal, The Lewis Legacy, The C.S. Lewis News (Ireland)*, several editions of the *Minister's Manual*, and others. He was a contributor to the best-selling *C.S. Lewis Readers' Encyclopedia* and the *Macmillan Encyclopedia of Science, Technology and Ethics*. Perry is currently writing a biography of William Lindsay Gresham and articles on Lewis, Tolkien and spirituality for several magazines and journals.

He is a graduate of Southern Seminary in Louisville, Kentucky, and a former pastor. Perry lives in Louisville with his wife, Joan, a nurse practitioner.

INTRODUCTION

From 1979 to 1993, scholars of C.S. Lewis gathered their work under the leadership and passion of the late Stephen L. Schofield, the founding publisher and editor of the now-defunct *Canadian C.S. Lewis Journal*. The result was described by *Eternity* magazine as "a sprightly, sometimes feisty newsletter." It was true. The collection of essays ran the gamut from the profoundly analytical to the unexpectedly hilarious. From 1993 to 2001, the *Journal* continued under the capable editorship of Roger Stronstad.

As delighted as we were by our own research and discoveries and as much as we delighted Stephen and each other—we were always more pleased to share our work with Lewisian aficionados worldwide. *Beyond Aslan* is our offering to you. In it, we have selected a wide range of topics and styles, all exploring some little-known aspect of C.S. Lewis that will deepen your understanding of his work and introduce you to the man he was. Some of us knew him personally or studied with him, so the insights are unique.

You'll notice that even though many of the essays are written by men and women with academic interest in Lewis's work, there are pieces written simply to tickle your fancy, such as the piece on the opinions of eight-year-olds, who have quite a lot to say. You'll even find an essay written by Lewis's stepson, Douglas Gresham, who offers you a personal glimpse into life in the Lewis household.

At the end of each essay, we introduce you to the scholar who wrote it, and he or she gives you source material so that you can read more on your own.

We also have *The Beyond Aslan Album*, a section of photos from The Marion E. Wade Centre, Wheaton College in Illinois (where the wardrobe from *The Lion, the Witch and the Wardrobe* is still in residence!) and photos from our own personal collections.

I wish to express thanks and appreciation to the essayists for granting permission to use their material, the staff at Bridge-Logos for their professionalism, Perry Bramlett for writing the Foreword amid a hectic schedule, and Roger Stronstad for providing appropriate photos.

We invite you now into the world of C.S. Lewis and many of the characters that occupied his books and his life.

– Burton K. Janes, Editor

BURTON K. JANES

Burton K. Janes was born in St. John's, Newfoundland, in 1957. A graduate of Memorial University of Newfoundland, St. John's (B.A., Religious Studies; M.A., History) and Eastern Pentecostal Bible College (now Master's College and Seminary), Peterborough, Ontario (now Toronto, Ontario), he holds ministerial credentials with the Pentecostal Assemblies of Newfoundland. He has served in a variety of pastoral capacities.

Burton is Archivist with the Pentecostal Assemblies of Newfoundland and Managing Editor of its official publication, *Good Tidings*. He is the owner/operator of Edit-Write. He is adjunct lecturer with Master's College and Seminary, and has been guest lecturer with the Religious Studies Department of Memorial University of Newfoundland.

He has written several books, including the two-volume biography of the founder of the Pentecostal Assemblies of Newfoundland, the American Alice B. Garrigus, *The Lady Who Came* and *The Lady Who Stayed*. He wrote his first book, *A Russian Adventure*, after winning a trip to the former Soviet Union in 1978. He wrote *History of the*

Pentecostal Assemblies of Newfoundland and, with the late John Parsons, *The King of Baffin Land: W. Ralph Parsons, Last Fur Trade Commissioner of the Hudson's Bay Company*. He has contributed to several books, including the *Encyclopedia of Newfoundland and Labrador*, *Dictionary of Newfoundland and Labrador Biography*, *We Remember C.S. Lewis: Essays and Memoirs* (ed., David Graham), and *Churches of Newfoundland and Labrador*, volumes 1 and 2. He is the author of four (to date) books in the History of Churches Series. He has edited scores of books. He has written numerous articles and book reviews for a variety of publications. He is a voracious reader with eclectic reading tastes. He is currently writing several books, including a biography of Samuel A.B. Mercer (1879-1969), the Egyptologist and Orientalist.

From 1993 to 2001 Burton assisted Roger Stronstad at various times as Associate Editor, Book Review Editor, and Consulting Editor of *The Canadian C.S. Lewis Journal*.

Burton and his wife, Sherry, live in Bay Roberts, Newfoundland, Canada. They have two grown children, Krista and Christopher. Burton's "shadow" is a black-and-white border collie by the name of Madisyn.

Beyond Aslan Album

CLIVE STAPLES LEWIS
as a student at Oxford, 1919.

Lewis family and staff on Little Lea steps, 1905. (Little Lea was the name given to the Lewis's house in Hillsborough.) *From l. to r.*, first row: Warren Lewis, C.S. Lewis, Leonard Lewis (cousin), and Eileen Lewis (cousin). *Second row*: Agnes Young Lewis (aunt), maid, maid, Flora Hamilton Lewis (mother), and Albert Lewis (father) holding the dog Nero.

The deer park, Magdalen College, Oxford. New Building where Lewis had his rooms is in the background.

The Eagle and Child, known also as Bird and Babe (or Baby) was the Oxford pub where the Inklings met on Tuesday mornings from 1939 until 1962.

Eastgate Hotel in Oxford, across the street from Magdalen College. Lewis had lunch with Joy Davidman and Phyllis Williams there on 24 September 1952.

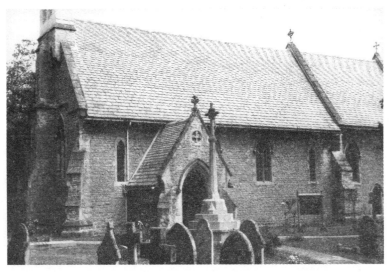

Holy Trinity Church in Headington Quarry, Lewis's parish church about a mile from the Kilns.

Magdalen College, Oxford University, where Lewis was a Fellow from 1925 to 1954.

Magdalene College, where Lewis became a Fellow upon becoming professor of Medieval and Renaissance English at Cambridge in 1954.

The Kilns, Lewis's home in the Oxford suburb of Headington Quarry in the southeast section of the city.

Some of the Inklings group, Trout Inn, Oxford, ca. 1940. *L. to r.*: Commander Jim Dundas-Grant, Colin Hardie, Dr. H.E. "Humphrey" Havard, C.S. Lewis, and Peter Havard (Dr. Havard's son).

Lewis in his study at "the Kilns."

Used by permission of The Marion E. Wade Center, Wheaton College, Wheaton, IL.

Joy Davidman Gresham, Lewis's wife, in 1960.

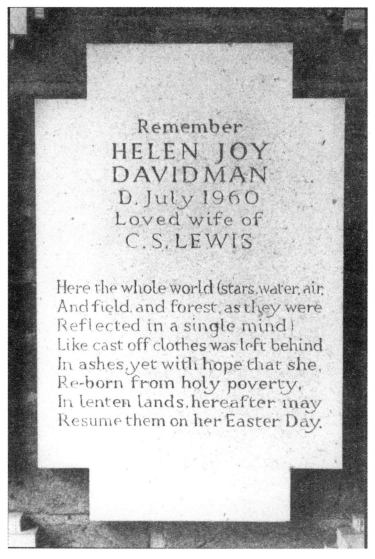

Remember
HELEN JOY
DAVIDMAN
D. July 1960
Loved wife of
C. S. LEWIS

Here the whole world (stars, water, air,
And field, and forest, as they were
Reflected in a single mind)
Like cast off clothes was left behind
In ashes, yet with hope that she,
Re-born from holy poverty,
In lenten lands, hereafter may
Resume them on her Easter Day.

Lewis's memorial plaque to his wife, Joy, now carved on her tomb.

Conferment of Honorary Degrees by the Chancellor

**The Right Honourable The Earl of Woolton,
C.H., P.C., D.L., LL.D.**

Presenter: Professor R. A. C. Oliver

Doctor of Laws

SIR VINCENT ZIANI DE FERRANTI
DR. HAROLD WILLIS DODDS
LADY EWING
SIR WILLIAM HENRY PILKINGTON

Doctor of Letters

PROFESSOR CLIVE STAPLES LEWIS

Doctor of Science

PROFESSOR SIR JAMES GRAY

Reply by

Dr. Harold W. Dodds

The Formula of Dismissal

Salva sit Universitas nostra Mancuniensis:
hoc precantes consurgamus

The National Anthem

(The Congregation is requested to join)

The Procession, led by the Chancellor, will leave the Hall

*(The Congregation will remain standing until the
Chancellor's Procession has left the Hall)*

3 1125-5-59

The program featuring Lewis receiving an honourary degree from
the University of Manchester.

Lewisiana

C.S. LEWIS: MERE CHRISTIAN

By Roger J. Stronstad

In 1947 his picture appeared on the cover of *Time* magazine above the subscription: OXFORD'S C.S. LEWIS. His heresy: Christianity. Since then the titles of several books have identified this Oxford don in terms of his faith: *C.S. Lewis: Mere Christian* (Lindskoog, 1973), and *A Christian for All Christians* (Walter and Patrick, eds., 1990). Other titles identify him as a Christian apologist: *Apostle to the Skeptics* (Walsh, 1949) and *Defender of the Faith* (Cunningham, 1967). Still others identify some particular aspect of his Christian thought: *Images of Salvation in the Fiction of C.S. Lewis* (Kilby, 1978). Through the Socratic Club, lectures to the Royal Air Force during World War II, sermons, radio talks, and, most of all, through his books, C.S. Lewis has become arguably the most influential Christian of the twentieth-first century.

C.S. Lewis's great influence in this century is as improbable as Paul's in the first century. By his midteens Lewis was an atheist, writing to a friend, "I believe in no religion." To Lewis, "All religions ... are merely man's own invention—Christ as much as Loki." He asserted further: "Often, too, great men were regarded as gods after their death ... thus after the death of a Hebrew philosopher Yeshua (whose name we have corrupted into Jesus), he became regarded as a god" (*TST* 135). After Lewis went up to Oxford as a student, however, a variety of influences conspired to undermine the uncritical atheism of his youth.

The long process which ultimately led to Lewis's conversion to Christianity actually began shortly before he attended Oxford. On one of his trips between his home in Ireland and England he bought and read George MacDonald's fantasy, *Phantastes*. This fairy tale by the nineteenth-century Christian Scottish novelist converted, even baptized, Lewis's imagination and in the reading of it he had crossed a great frontier, which ultimately led to Christianity. In reading G.K. Chesterton later, as in reading MacDonald, Lewis did not know what he was letting himself in for— "more sense than all other moderns put together" (*SJ* 213). In retrospect Lewis the Christian observed: "A young man who wishes to remain a sound atheist cannot be too careful of his reading. There are traps everywhere" (*SJ* 191).

At Oxford Lewis excelled as a student, taking a "first" in three disciplines: classics, philosophy and English literature. To his surprise he met a number of other intelligent students who were Christians. He even met an atheist who seemed to accept the historic claims of Christianity, saying: "Rum thing. It (i.e., the death and resurrection of a god) almost looks as if it had really happened once." But not only did he meet intelligent students at Oxford who were Christians, after he became a tutor he also met intelligent colleagues, such as J.R.R. Tolkien, who were Christians.

Through these and other influences the Hound of Heaven pursued him. Night after night in his rooms in Magdalen College he felt, he reports,

> … the steady unrelenting approach of Him whom I so earnestly desired not to meet. … In the Trinity Term of 1929 I gave in, and admitted that God was God, and knelt and prayed: perhaps, that night, the most dejected and reluctant convert in all England" (*SJ* 228-29).

But this was only a conversion to theism–the belief in God. Two more years would pass before he converted to Christianity, finally seeing: "Here and here only in all time the myth must have become fact; the Word, flesh; God, Man" (*SJ* 236). In other words, he came to believe that Jesus Christ was the Son of God (*SJ* 237).

Within two years of his conversion he published an autobiographical allegory, *The Pilgrim's Regress: An Allegorical Apology for Christianity, Reason and Romanticism* (1933). This was modeled after John Bunyan's great allegory, *The Pilgrim's Progress*. This autobiography emphasizes the subjective aspects of his spiritual pilgrimage—the recurrent experience of intense longing, which he called variously Romanticism, or *Sensucht*, or joy. This stabbing pain of desire is not satisfied by any earthy object. It, therefore, points to an object beyond this world (i.e., to God) for its fulfillment. This intense longing gives its name to a second, non-allegorical biography, *Surprised by Joy: The Shape of My Early Life* (1955).

Lewis was a thoroughly converted atheist. It is, therefore, no surprise that the Space trilogy, which he published between 1938 and 1945 reflects a thoroughly Christian mind-set. These novels, in fact, recapitulate themes from Genesis 1-11 in science fiction form: *Out of the Silent Planet* (1938) recapitulates themes from Genesis 2; *Perelandra (Voyage to Venus)* [1943] retells Genesis 3, but with a happy ending; and *That Hideous Strength: A Modern Fairy-Tale for Grown-Ups* (1945) has its own Tower of Babel/confusion of languages scene (Genesis 11). The significance of the name of the hero of the stories, Ransom, will not be lost on readers who are familiar with the Bible. At one level Lewis was motivated to write these novels simply to get more of the kind of stories which he enjoyed reading. At another level, he was opposing the atheist "dream of interplanetary colonization"—one of the "scientific" hopes for defeating death (*Letters* 167). Thus, these novels are tools for the evangelization of England.

The war years catapulted this very private Oxford don into national and eventually worldwide public notice. In 1940 he published *The Problem of Pain* in the Christian Challenge Series. Soon he was invited to preach. Sermons such as "The Weight of Glory" (1941) and "Transposition" (1944) had a stunning effect on audiences. Beginning in the Fall of 1941 he traveled throughout England on weekends to Royal Air Force bases to address the airmen, many of whom would soon die in the defense of their country. In 1942 he gave the first of a series of radio broadcast talks, "Right and Wrong as a Clue to the Meaning of the Universe." This was followed by three more series:

"What Christians Believe," "Christian Behaviour," and "Beyond Personality: or First Steps in the Doctrine of the Trinity." These broadcast talks were collected and published in 1952 as the now classic book of Christian apologetics, *Mere Christianity*. At the same time the Socratic Club was formed, with Lewis as the founding president. It was formed to debate the pros and cons of the Christian religion and *Who's Who* was consulted to find intelligent atheists who had both the inclination and the time to enter into the arena with Lewis, the converted atheist, and others. Also in 1942, the Screwtape letters were published in book form. Though Lewis did, in fact, believe in a personal devil, and though the letters are from a senior tempter, Screwtape, to a novice tempter, Wormwood, the book is really not about the devil. It is about the psychology of temptation and the sinfulness of the human heart, and it is for this reason one of his most popular books.

During the War Lewis accepted into his home a number of children who were evacuated out of war-ravaged London. The presence of these children of various ages inspired the fifty-two-year-old bachelor to pull together various "pictures"—of a faun carrying an umbrella, of a lion whom he named Aslan, etc.—and write a children's story, published in 1950 as *The Lion, the Witch and the Wardrobe*. Six more stories set in the fairy tale land of Narnia were soon published. At one level these deal with "growing up" (and even adult) issues of trust, truthfulness, valour, obedience, character development, and much more. At another level the Narnia Chronicles are tools of pre-evangelism. They give to children important aspects of Christian doctrine in imaginative narrative form to enable them to recognize and understand them better when they encounter them in the Bible. For example, in *The Magician's Nephew* there is a creation scene, in *The Lion, the Witch and the Wardrobe* there are substitutionary sacrifice and resurrection episodes, and in *The Last Battle* the world of Narnia is brought to an end. But most important of all there is Aslan, the imaginative portrait of Christ.

This, in part, is the Lewis whose books had by 1994 sold over 100,000,000 copies. Forty plus years after his death in 1963, his popularity is, if anything, going forth from strength to strength. Yet he also has many Christian detractors. Some liberals don't like him because of his belief in the supernatural (i.e., miracles, the devil) and because of his Biblicism. Many fundamentalists don't like him because he drank beer, smoked cigarettes, and believed in purgatory. Those Christians who tend to emphasize reason in their faith are sometimes put off by Lewis's use of science fiction or children's fantasy to communicate Christian truth. So Lewis's books are not to everyone's taste. But by the million many, many Christians read with pleasure and profit the books of this man who wrote about Christianity with unparalleled reason and imagination.

Roger J. Stronstad

Roger J. Stronstad is professor of Bible and Theology at Summit Pacific College, Abbotsford, British Columbia. He is the author of numerous articles, reviews and several books. His books include *The Charismatic Theology of St. Luke* (Peabody: Hendrickson Publishers, 1984), *Spirit, Scripture and Theology: A Pentecostal Perspective* (Baguio City, Philippines: Asia Pacific Theological Seminary Press, 1995), and *The Prophethood of All Believers: A Study in Luke's Charismatic Theology* (Sheffield: Sheffield Academic Press, 1999). He is the editor, with Laurence M. Van Kleek, of *The Holy Spirit in the Scriptures and the Church: Essays presented to Leslie Thomas Holdcroft on his 65th Birthday* (Clayburn, British Columbia/Sumas, Washington: Western Pentecostal Bible College, 1987). He is an avid reader of the books by and about these writers called the Inklings, their friends and their predecessors. Following the death in 1993 of Stephen Schofield, publisher of *The Canadian C.S. Lewis Journal*, Roger published and edited the *Journal* until its final issue, No. 100, Autumn 2001. He is currently a member of the Advisory Board of the journal *SEVEN: An Anglo-American Literary Review*.

WORKS CITED

- *Letters. Letters of C.S. Lewis*, edited, with a memoir, by W.H. Lewis (New York: Harcourt, Brace and World, Inc., 1966).

- *SJ. Surprised by Joy: The Shape of My Early Life*, by C.S. Lewis (New York: Harcourt, Brace and Company, 1956).

- *TST. They Stand Together*, edited by Walter Hooper (London: Collins, 1979).

C.S. Lewis and Weather

By Evan K. Gibson

C.S. Lewis was a man remarkably sensitive to natural beauty—in fact, pleased with all the moods of nature. Like the Dennistons in *That Hideous Strength: A Modern Fairy-Tale for Grown-Ups*, he liked "weather." Writing to Joseph Arthur Greeves, his lifelong friend, Lewis observes: "That is a thing you and I have to be thankful for—the fact that we not only don't dislike but positively enjoy almost every kind of weather." As his letters indicate, it did not matter whether it was the pearl gray sky- of an autumn evening, a "glorious" storm in which the trees plunged "like terrified but tethered horses," or the ground fog of a winter morning which reduced all objects to neutral shades and silhouettes. He simply liked weather.

The frequent walking tours, some in January with his brother, Warnie, others in spring or autumn with Oxford friends, are often described in letters. While still a student, C.S. Lewis wrote in 1921 of a walk around Standlake in Oxfordshire. He speaks of a "long and pleasant decline through corkscrew lanes full of meadow sweet," and comments on the "warm and muffled" countryside which makes you feel "like a bumble bee that has got into damp cotton wool."

In 1935, now a don of Magdalen College, Lewis wrote to Greeves of a walking tour with Arthur Owen Barfield and others in Derbyshire. He speaks of it as much "like my ideal country." The limestone mountains made for a jagged skyline and deep valleys, but the paleness of the rock and the extreme clarity of the rivers made it "*light* instead of somber—sublime yet smiling—like the delectable mountains."

But it is not only on walking tours that Lewis shows his sensitivity to nature. His letters often display the influence of its daily moods. He writes from his home at the Kilns of "a lovely walk in the afternoon—a perfect winter day with mellow sunlight slanting through a half frosty mist on the grey fields, the cosy farms, and tall, leafless elms, absolutely unmoving in the air."

This letter illustrates Lewis's special enjoyment of winter. He describes himself as having the constitution of a polar bear. And like a polar bear he shows the least enthusiasm for the heat of summer. Autumn, however, was another season in which he delighted. On an October day he speaks of "a white liquid sky with horizontal bands of darker grey and a white sun behind them. Not a breath of wind." In November he writes of "lovely sunrise through tall elms twinkling over the frosty grass this morning."

Lewis did not believe, however, that the countryside should be appreciated in its beautiful moods only. It was his friend, Alfred Kenneth Hamilton Jenkin, who taught him that it is possible to enjoy what others would call the ugly aspects of nature—to delight in the quiddity of things. On a dismal day, Lewis says, "find the most dismal and dripping wood." Immerse yourself in her grimness. Whatever quality nature is showing at the moment, recognize it as one of her multitudinous faces. Such an attitude was sometimes useful on the walking tours when fog or rain spoiled an expected enjoyment of a sweeping prospect.

But when Lewis advises us to immerse ourselves in nature's grimness or gaiety—whichever face she offers—he is not saying with Wordsworth, "Let nature be your teacher." In fact, he is saying almost the opposite. "Nature," he says in *The Four Loves*, "will teach you exactly the lessons you have already decided to learn." The convinced materialist will find his materialism reinforced, the convinced mystic, his mysticism. To the man of faith the heavens declare the glory of God. To the agnostic they declare only the enigma of questions without answers.

Nature does not teach, says Lewis. Like the wind which surrounds every boulder and presses into every crevice and yet has no shape of its own, nature showers us with images which we can use in expressing our faith, but offers nothing more. Our beliefs must come from another source. For that, he says, we must return "to our studies, to church, to our Bibles, to our knees."

There may be hints of the Creator in the blazing suns which bediamond our night from unimaginable distances, or in the creeping pelt of grass which clothes the naked scalp of the earth. After all, the image of the artist is, in some sense, always in his handiwork. But it is there only in some sense. There are too many tangles (as we see it) in the history of the universe for the image of the artist to be seen clearly.

The flawless mirror, Lewis would say, is to be found in the incarnation—God made flesh in Christ. Once you have seen that, nature will offer you its resources for the language you wish to use to describe that image. Again, in *The Four Loves* he says, "nature never taught me that there existed a God of glory and of infinite majesty. I had to learn that in other ways. But nature gave the word glory a meaning for me. I still do not know where else I could have found one."

We should also note that Lewis did not regard natural beauty as a quality completely divorced from human endeavour. He expresses his enjoyment of delightful villages, of old country churches with their square pews, and of "a quaint old inn that might have stepped out of *The Vicar of Wakefield.*"[1] Writing to Arthur Greeves, Lewis shares a walk through falling snow down a village street past the blacksmith shop, "and you could see the red forge glowing inside." Although the sprawling city was not to his taste, Lewis's countryside was one to which man had contributed, often giving it character and meaning.

That nature also contributes to man and ministers to his needs C.S. Lewis had numerous reminders, some of which seem to have crept into his tales. The relationship of factual England to the multicolored universe of his imagination is that of raindrop to rainbow—the mundane drizzle transformed to a glorious arch reaching beyond the horizon. We must assume, therefore, that soil and grass in common sunlight and ordinary rain were the materials out of which Lewis shaped, at least in part, the lands of his fiction.

---

1. *The Vicar of Wakefield* by Oliver Goldsmith.

EVAN K. GIBSON (1909-93)

It was in mid-career that Evan K. Gibson became acquainted with the writings of C.S. Lewis that were to so profoundly impact his thinking for the remainder of his life. At the time, he was teaching English Literature at Oregon State University and found himself challenged to defend his life-long Christian faith through an analytical process that seemed to pit his most cherished tenets of faith against his own intellectual honesty. And it was in the midst of this very personal Reason vs. Faith struggle that he came across the book, *Mere Christianity*, and was thus introduced to its author, C.S. Lewis. Here he had found a kindred soul, an academic colleague who was addressing the same questions and doubts and, more importantly, had been able to articulate a rationale for the Christian faith by means of objective, scholarly reasoning. This proved to be a lifeline to Gibson, pulling him onto shore where there was solid, "intellectual-spiritual" ground, and it was possible to "give a reason for the hope that is within you." And there, like Lewis—and, to a large extent, *because* of Lewis—he found substantial footing for both intellectual objectivity and spiritual experience.

During his career, Gibson authored many articles for scholarly and religious periodicals. He maintained his keen interest in C.S. Lewis, writing the book, *C.S. Lewis: Spinner of Tales* (1980), and participating as a presenter at the "C.S. Lewis Institute" conferences held at Seattle Pacific University.

To his family, it seemed a very fitting memorial to Gibson's Christian faith and his debt of gratitude to Lewis that a quote from *The Last Battle* be inscribed on his memorial stone—after Gibson's own "last battle" with cancer ended in 1993— "The dream is ended: this is the morning."

HUMOUR AND SPIRITUALITY: CHEERFUL GIVERS

By *Darin Harootunian*

The cheer and humour which pervade the serious spiritual themes in the works of G.K. Chesterton and C.S. Lewis are unusual qualities in religious writings. The success of these two men in maintaining the humorous with the serious is certainly due to their individual genius and skill as writers, but to leave the explanation for their success at this level is to say nothing beyond the apparent. There is no dispute that both these men on occasion were very formidable wits, but there is something much larger at work in their writings, something common to both men which affords them the ease of speaking very plainly about themselves and their faith. Perhaps the humour with which these men speak of religious matters stems from the irony in their particular journeys to faith, from the abandonment of the religion and tradition of their fathers to the arrival at the very place from which they fled. It certainly is no new story to Christendom, but it does go a long way in explaining the lives and works of both Chesterton and Lewis.

Chesterton likened his journey to Christian orthodoxy to that of an English yachtsman who set sail from his homeland but by a miscalculation in his course discovered England under the impression that it was an island in the South Sea. Such a man, said Chesterton, would be the victim of a very heroic and "enviable" mistake. He would enjoy on a single occasion "all the fascinating terrors of going abroad combined with all the humane security of coming home again" (*Orthodoxy*, p. 14). Chesterton writes,

> Nearly all people I have ever met in this western society in which I live would agree to the general proposition that we need this life of practical romance; the combination of something that is strange with something that is secure. We need to view the world as to combine an idea of wonder and an idea of welcome (p. 16).

For the westerner whose civilization is founded upon Christianity, this practical romance is at the heart of the Christian conversion; it involves both the joy of discovering some distant Land and the humour of learning that you have arrived in the very country from which you departed. For the Christian, it is often the first laugh of all real laughs, and it is the great laugh at oneself.

In Chesterton's novel, *The Man Who Was Thursday: A Nightmare*, Gabriel Syme, the philosophical policeman and poet of order, justice, and goodness, penetrates the Central Council of anarchists to expose and foil its attempts at destroying the world, but he discovers that the entire Council consists not of anarchists but of fellow philosophical policemen who like himself are commissioned to expose and extirpate the evil of anarchy. Stranger still, he discovers that even Sunday, the frightful Chief of the Council, was bent not upon destroying the world but upon bringing meaning and peace to it. Syme learns in the end that it was necessary for him to stand terrified and alone in the Council of Days in order for the claims of Satan to be revealed for the lies which they are. He had to suffer and endure the isolation, the glory and the freedom of the anarchist so that he too could earn the right to say to his accuser, "You Lie!" (p. 119).

In a sense, Syme is the English yachtsman who sailed for the South Seas but discovered the island of England; he penetrated the most fearsome and pernicious circle of men only to find its members consisting of his detective colleagues who also were charged with uncovering anarchy and preserving goodness, order and justice. He had to experience in a moment "all the fascinating terrors of going abroad combined with all the humane security of coming home again" in order that he could earn the right to say to himself, "You fool of fools! You set out to preserve civilization but ended up again in the 'Sunday' school of your youth. If you had learned your creeds and lessons the first time around, you would have saved yourself a great deal of agony." (Of course these latter lines are my own folly, that of giving words to someone else's character, but, if you will, let it stand—exposed for what it is—for the sake of my point.) This realization becomes for Syme an acknowledgment of his own ridiculousness. It is an acknowledgment that this is available to everyone but chosen only by a few.

In C.S. Lewis's *The Great Divorce: A Dream*, the character George MacDonald tells the story of Sir Archibald who in his earthly life was concerned in nothing but the survival and immortality of the soul. His interests at first were philosophical, but as they grew, he got involved in Psychical Research. He lectured, experimented, and traveled to Tibet and Central Africa gathering mystical stories and evidence for his proofs. During one of his country's wars, he got himself into trouble by running up and down the countryside calling for all the war funds to be poured into Research instead, but when Sir Archibald finally died and traveled to the outskirts of Heaven, he found the place very contrary to his interests. There was no need for his proofs of survival; everyone had already survived, and no one had any interest in the question. There was nothing in Heaven for him to do, and he had no reason or desire to stay. MacDonald says,

> Of course if he would only have admitted that he'd mistaken the means for the end and had a good laugh at himself he could have begun all over again like a little child and entered into joy. But he would not do that. He cared nothing about joy. In the end he went away (p.71).

When Sir Archibald learned that all his research and ideas were for naught, that his great discovery was no discovery at all, he did not admit his folly, laugh at himself, and start all over again as a child. He instead was bothered so much by the disinterest in the question and the lack of attention paid to him that he stormed out of Heaven indignant and perturbed. Perhaps it can be said that the story of Sir Archibald is the sad account of those who refuse to be made the fool even for their own good.

In *The Pilgrim's Regress: An Allegorical Apology for Christianity, Reason and Romanticism* (Lewis's allegorical account of his conversion to Christianity) the pilgrim John secretly sets out one night from his father's house in Puritania in search of a mysterious island whose vision awakened in him, *sweet desire*—an infinite longing. After traveling west from Puritania and the Landlord's Mountain through strange and dangerous lands (discovering such cities as Thrill and Eschropolis and meeting such men as Mr. Enlightenment and Mr. Humanist), he despairs and eventually gives himself up to Mother Kirk (or Christianity). Upon his resignation, Mother Kirk tells him, "It is well. You have come a long way around to reach this place, whither I would have carried you in a few moments. But it is very well" (Book IX, chapter 4). He soon learns that the Island of his desire is but the other side of the Landlord's Mountain, and the only way to reach the Mountain is to turn east, the very direction from which he came. Before John begins his regress, his guide tells him, "You may be sure the Landlord has brought you the shortest way; though I confess it would look an odd journey on a map" (Book IX, chapter 4). John's only response upon learning this news is, "what must be must be. I deserve no better." They are words spoken in solemn defeat without even a trace of humour. There were no concessions won for his surrender. There are still dragons to be fought and a long harrowing journey to be completed, but what he learns is far better than any conditions he could *ever* have negotiated: the victory is ensured. It is from this assurance that there grows a peace with which he can look upon the agonies of his crooked past with a faint smile. It seems very likely that the warm laughter and cheer found throughout Lewis's many works—from his fiction to his apologetics—spring from such a smile.

There is yet another reason for the success of these two men in uniting the humourous with the serious. In *Orthodoxy* Chesterton says that he takes as common ground between himself and his reader the "desirability of an active and imaginative life, picturesque and full of poetical curiosity, a life such as western man at any rate always seems to have desired" (p. 16). If any explanation is given for how Chesterton and Lewis succeed in introducing humour into the seriousness of their spiritual themes, it should involve, at least in part, this assumption concerning the "desirability of an active and imaginative life." The writings of both these men embody that "picturesque [life] full of poetical curiosity" which for the western mind is a welcome alternative to the distorted logic and forced simplicity of naturalism. The imaginative and poetic qualities found even in their philosophical and spiritual themes produce in the end a rich conversational tone that provides for the introduction of their great humour.

DARIN HAROOTUNIAN

Darin Harootunian is currently a graduate student in analytic philosophy. His essay, "Humour and Spirituality: Cheerful Givers," was written for a class conducted by Dr. Janice B. Brown at Grove City College, Grove City, Pennsylvania. He expresses special appreciation to Professor Brown for her thoughtful and rewarding class on Christian works of fiction, for her characteristic warmth and encouragement, and for her abundant patience (primarily with him).

THE SCREWTAPE LETTERS:
OF GREED AND GRACE

By Jack L. Knowles

hen the first American edition of *The Screwtape Letters* appeared in 1943, Leonard Bacon, writing in *The Saturday Review of Literature*, called it an "admirable...and remarkably original work ... a spectacular ... nova in a bleak sky of satire" (20). Not that the nova was born without pain—Lewis said writing *Screwtape* "produced a sort of spiritual cramp" (Preface to the paperback edition, *Screwtape*, xiv), and two years after it was published, he remarked that he would say no more about the devil as public association of author with demonic character was already too far along: "In some quarters," he said, "it has already reached the level of confusion if not of identification" (Gibson, 101).

In any case, the public was fascinated by the infernal correspondence. Arriving in book form in Britain in 1942, it went through nine printings in the first year, and it has since been translated into at least fifteen languages (Green and Hooper, 199-200) and has sold over two million copies worldwide (Sayer, 274). It was the kind of literary success that is most uncommon and most uncomfortable for an Oxford don. One of his biographers writes: "There is nothing like worldly success on the part of one academic to make all the others hate him or her" (Wilson, 181).

What sort of literature is this book? If not absolutely *sui generis*, it's at least rather strange, isn't it? Few literary efforts seem to be close relatives. And yet, for all of its infernal strangeness, it gives us glimpses into the human condition. What does it tell us about being human?

Let's take the literary issue first. On the one hand *Screwtape* is a kind of epistolary novel—a piece of fiction in which the story is told through letters. As such it is a distant relative of Samuel Richardson's eighteenth-century novel *Pamela*, but unlike that lengthy tome (whose bulk led to the oft-repeated quip, "*Pamela*'s a million laughs—one every other page"), the story line of *Screwtape* is pretty slight and could be summed up in a few sentences. It follows part of the adult life of Wormwood's "patient," who becomes a Christian, resists a number of temptations, falls in love, and dies when his city is bombed. But it's not the events, it's the ideas that keep our attention. And those ideas are introduced and played with primarily through the vehicle of satire.

One of the first things we notice when we analyze *Screwtape* as a satire is that, like the great eighteenth-century satirist Jonathan Swift in *A Modest Proposal*, Lewis deftly creates a well-educated, urbane man-of-the-world as the book's persona (spokesdevil, if you prefer). Like that of Swift's persona, Screwtape's thoughtful, sophisticated tone belies a fundamental viciousness. Lewis warns us in the original preface that Screwtape's assessment of things is not to be trusted, and yet it's easy for us to be lulled into uncritical acceptance of what he has to say. If we're alert, we'll pick up the stiletto thrusts beneath the calm tone of this advice in Letter V:

> My dear Wormwood,
>
> It is a little bit disappointing to expect a detailed report on your work and to receive instead such a vague rhapsody as your last letter. You say you are "delirious with joy" because the European humans have started another of their wars. I see very well what has happened to you. You are not delirious; you are only drunk. Reading between the lines in your very

unbalanced account of the patient's sleepless night, I can reconstruct your state of mind fairly accurately. For the first time in your career you have tasted that wine which is the reward of all our labours—the anguish and bewilderment of a human soul—and it has gone to your head (24-25).

The thrusts are in phrases like "vague rhapsody" and "very unbalanced account." Later we'll catch glimpses of Screwtape's naked hatred, fear, and, at the end, ravenous greed.

In one crucial scene, in Letter XXII, Lewis uses an allusion to another infernal adventure, Milton's *Paradise Lost*, to remind us forcefully that Screwtape lacks credibility. Having learned that Wormwood's patient has fallen in love, and with a Christian, Screwtape boils over with fury at the thought that the beloved, this "Filthy, insipid little prude" (101), has the gall to find Screwtape, himself, laughable. When he turns his fury towards Wormwood, Screwtape is suddenly transformed:

> Meanwhile *you*, disgusting little—
>
> [*Here the MS. breaks off and is resumed in a different hand.*]
>
> In the heat of composition I find that I have inadvertently allowed myself to assume the form of a large centipede. I am accordingly dictating the rest to my secretary [Toadpipe]. Now that the transformation is complete, I recognize it as a periodical phenomenon. Some rumour of it has reached the humans, and a distorted account of it appears in the poet Milton, with the ridiculous addition that such changes of shape are a "punishment" imposed on us by the Enemy (103).

The allusion is to Book 10 of *Paradise Lost*, where Satan returns to hell and proudly tells his cohorts how he has deceived Adam and Eve. Expecting thunderous applause, he hears instead thunderous hissing and realizes that all of the troops have been turned into snakes. He doesn't have long to wonder, however, because, in Milton's words:

> His arms clung to his ribs, his legs entwining
> Each other, till, supplanted, down he fell

A monstrous serpent on his belly prone,
Reluctant, but in vain; a greater power
Now ruled him, punished in the shape he sinned,
According to his doom (512-517).

What's the significance of this allusion? I think Lewis expects us to remember that Satan's metamorphosis was quite certainly a punishment meted out by "a greater power." If we do remember this scene in Milton, we then see that Screwtape is a liar when he claims that his own change is something that he has "inadvertently allowed." The scene is one of many reminders that we better not swallow uncritically what Screwtape has to say, lest we ourselves be swallowed by his ravenous appetite.

Much of the satire comes, then, through Lewis's handling of his debonair but deadly persona. But the satire is also built into the very structure and processes of the hell that Screwtape represents. When we learn that the operatives in the infernal regions care only about the accomplishment of the goals mandated by their supervisors and are not at all bothered by the fact that individuals are crushed in the process, we recognize a satirical picture of the modern bureaucratic state—the Infernal Revenue Service, if you will. Fifteen years ago I received a letter from the Internal Revenue Service on December 9 informing me that I was required to carry out a charter revision for a charitable organization I represented, and that the revised charter, complete with state approval, had to be returned to the IRS office in Atlanta no later than December 8. My attempts to gain an extension, given the difficulty of revising our charter by yesterday, were entirely futile. Because many have experienced such frustrations, we can identify with Lewis's satire of the faceless, bureaucratic web, a satire which may remind us of the deadly governmental octopus pictured in Franz Kafka's novel *The Trial*, published just four years before *Screwtape*'s first appearance.

Unlike Kafka's picture, however, Lewis's satire is frequently humourous. There is humour in the reversal of terminology, so that Satan is "Our Father Below," who rules over a vast "Lowerarchy." Screwtape glows with approval of the patient's new friends, who are "thoroughly reliable people; steady, consistent scoffers" (49). But he fulminates against the family of the patient's beloved, a family built on the principle of "disinterested love," or, in Screwtape's words, "one vast obscenity" (102).

Lewis, the literary and philosophical scholar, plays with this reversal of language not only for laughs, but also because he believed, like Socrates, that a sloppy or corrupt use of language could have catastrophic consequences. Thus when *Puritanism* has been distorted to mean simply the hatred of pleasure or "the haunting fear that someone, somewhere, may be happy" (Mencken, 239), Screwtape can chortle with glee, "the value we have given to that word is one of the really solid triumphs of the last hundred years[.] By it we rescue annually thousands of humans from temperance, chastity, and sobriety of life" (47). When *democracy* has been transformed into a conviction that everyone ought to be equal in all areas of life, then every attempt at excellence is cut down to size. Valedictorian honours and accelerated classes are eliminated as offensive examples of elitism, and society pursues feel-good-about-yourself mediocrity (an idea that Lewis develops at some length in *Screwtape Proposes a Toast*, 161-163 and 165-167).

What does all of this satire tell us about the nature of humanity? Well, at no place in *Screwtape* or anywhere else does Lewis give us a comprehensive, theoretical analysis of human nature, and I'm sure that's intentional. He was convinced that part of what makes us human is the possession of mind/spirit, and this aspect of our being doesn't fit the categories of natural science. To insist on studying humans simply like chemical reactions or even like non-human organisms is reductionism. It ignores or denies what doesn't fit into its categories (Holmer, 70-72). It's like a mathematician denying the existence of love because there is no geometric proof by which one can demonstrate the existence of love: "It doesn't fit my system of argumentation; therefore, it doesn't exist."

So Lewis doesn't try to define human nature. Instead, he tries to show us human individuals, especially in his fiction. What does he show us in *Screwtape*? For one thing, he reveals how quick we are to judge each other on the basis of trivialities. According to Screwtape, if the patient's "neighbours sing out of tune, or have boots that squeak, or double chins, or odd clothes, [he] will quite easily believe that their religion must therefore be somehow ridiculous" (12). While we are quick to judge others, we are frequently blind to our own faults. Thus Screwtape is delighted by "that most useful human characteristic, the horror and neglect of the obvious," which enables the patient to "practice self-examination for an hour without discovering any of those facts about himself which are perfectly clear to anyone who has ever lived in the same house with him or worked in the same office" (16).

Screwtape also sees in Wormwood's patient what he calls the "Law of Undulation"—a life of emotional and spiritual peaks and valleys. He explains: "Humans are amphibians—half spirit and half animal.... This means that while their spirit can be directed to an eternal object, their bodies, passions, and imaginations are in continual change, for to be in time means to change" (36-37). Nonetheless, we frequently act as if our present condition (whether joyful or depressed) is permanent. It's evident in our athletic contests, in the broadcaster's favourite friend, "momentum." When everything is going right (or wrong), it just seems like we're invincible (or incompetent). Anybody who has ever been "in a zone" on the tennis courts or struggled with depression in the living room knows how permanent that condition feels.

And yet, ironically, we're at other times obsessed by change. The master tempter Screwtape finds an additional weakness to exploit in humanity's belief in phases. He urges Wormwood to directly attack his patient's faith by convincing "him that 'his religious phase' is just going to die away like all his previous phases[.] Of course," Screwtape admits,

> ... there is no conceivable way of getting by reason from the proposition "I am losing interest in this" to the proposition "This is false." But, as I said before, it is jargon, not reason, you must rely on. The mere word *phase* will very likely do the trick. I assume that the creature has been through several of them before—they all have—and that he always feels superior and patronizing to the ones he has emerged from, not because he has really criticized them but simply because they are in the past (43).

When we climb to junior high status, power rangers are hopelessly stupid. Once we reach high school, we can't believe what nerds we were in junior high (and we look with pity or scorn on the hopeless little junior high brutes beneath us). And so it is with our view of faded interests that have little to do with age—whether it's bowling, gardening, line dancing, euchre, or, argues Screwtape, religion. It's so pleasant to recognize how superior we are to all those people who are still interested in what interests us no longer. Lewis would wake us up to the fact that none of this phase consciousness—nor its relative, our "horror of the Same Old Thing" (116)—has much to do with the crucial issues of Truth and Falsehood. It's just one more manifestation of "the law of Undulation."

Another human characteristic which the patient illustrates is the desire to fit in, especially to fit in to some kind of inner ring in society (the dreaded power of peer pressure). When Lewis's patient meets the well-educated, clever, fashionable, middle-aged skeptics, he's swept along with the tide. Screwtape notes that playing a false social game can have enduring consequences, since "[a]ll mortals tend to turn into the thing they are pretending to be" (46). And he recommends to Wormwood that most powerful of all modern social games, "flippancy"— the sly refusal to take anything seriously: "Only a clever human can make a real Joke about virtue, or indeed about anything else," advises the senior devil;

> ... any of them can be trained to talk *as if* virtue were funny. Among flippant people the Joke is always assumed to have been made. No one actually makes it; but every serious subject is discussed in a manner which implies that they have already found a ridiculous side to it. If prolonged, the habit of Flippancy builds up around a man the finest armour plating against the Enemy that I know, and it is quite free from the dangers inherent in the other sources of laughter. It is a thousand miles away from joy; it deadens, instead of sharpening, the intellect; and it excites no affection between those who practise it (52).

The human intellect has also been deadened by "the Historical Point of View." Screwtape explains that apparently innocuous phrase as follows:

> ... when a learned man is presented with any statement by an ancient author, the one question he never asks is whether it is

true. He asks who influenced the ancient writer, and how far the statement is consistent with what is said in other books, and what phase in the writer's development, or in the general history of thought, it illustrates, and how it affected later writers, and how often it has been misunderstood (specially by the learned man's own colleagues) and what the general course of criticism on it has been for the last ten years, and what is the "present state of the question." To regard the ancient writer as a possible source of knowledge—to anticipate that what he said could possibly modify your thoughts or your behaviour—this would be rejected as unutterably simple-minded (128-129).

But we must remember that the speaker of those words is Screwtape, and his picture of this "vile slime," otherwise known as a human being, is skewed. In fact, for all of his follies, Wormwood's patient ultimately acts with faithful courage in the midst of the carnage of war. And so he meets death, the great clarifier, with grace. Screwtape burns with envious anger as he writes:

The more one thinks about it, the worse it becomes. He got through so easily! No gradual misgivings, no doctor's sentence, no nursing home, no operating theatre, no false hopes of life: sheer, instantaneous liberation. One moment it seemed to be all our world; the scream of bombs, the fall of houses, the stink and taste of high explosive on the lips and in the lungs, the feet burning with weariness, the heart cold with horrors, the brain reeling, the legs aching; next moment all this was gone, gone like a bad dream, never again to be of any account (146).

Screwtape turns his wrath on Wormwood:

Defeated, outmanoeuvred fool! Did you mark how naturally—as if he'd been born for it—the Earthborn vermin entered the new life? How all his doubts became, in the twinkling of an eye, ridiculous? ...

As he saw you, he also saw Them. I know how it was. You reeled back dizzy and blinded, more hurt by them than he had ever been by bombs. The degradation of it!—that this thing of earth and slime could stand upright and converse with spirits before whom you, a spirit, could only cower (146-147).

As the book ends, the bitter stench of Screwtape's hatred and gnawing greed is almost overpowering—almost, but not quite, because ultimately Screwtape's malodorous fury serves only to contrast with and to emphasize the sweet smell of divine grace that envelops the patient as he meets the messengers of Truth. The epistolary novel ends with an epiphany; the satire, with celebration.

JACK L. KNOWLES

Jack L. Knowles earned his B.A. from Milligan College, Tennessee, and his M.A. and Ph.D. in English from the University of Tennessee, with specialties in seventeenth-century English drama and nineteenth-century American literature.

Since 1970 he has taught at Milligan College, where he currently serves as Professor of English and Chair of the Area of Humane Learning. He has taught extensively in Milligan's interdisciplinary Humanities Program, which examines the development of Western culture from the perspectives of history, literature, philosophy, and fine arts. His upper-division courses have included Restoration and Eighteenth-Century Literature, Eighteenth- and Nineteenth-Century Novel, American Literature to the Late Nineteenth Century, Elizabethan Drama, Jacobean Drama, and English Renaissance Poetry and Prose. In 2004 he was awarded the *Fide et Amore* Distinguished Service Citation by Milligan College.

In 1992 Dr. Knowles spent a sabbatical leave at the University of Oxford. During the Michaelmas Term, he did research at the Bodleian Library and attended the weekly meetings of the Oxford C.S. Lewis Society on Tuesday evenings. Among the outgrowths of the sabbatical was his participation as one of several featured speakers at the C.S. Lewis Festival in Kingsport, Tennessee, in February 1995. That in turn led to his publication of an article analyzing Lewis's *Screwtape Letters* in the Autumn 1996 issue of *The Canadian C.S. Lewis Journal*. In addition, he has enjoyed teaching a course on The Fiction of C.S. Lewis on a regular basis at Milligan College since 1993, delighted with the enthusiastic response from his students.

Dr. Knowles has published articles on seventeenth-century English drama, the Great Books, and fantasy literature, as well as C.S. Lewis. He has led several extensive study tours of Europe, taken part in a three-week seminar (focused on the question, "What is an American?") at the National Humanities Centre, and played an active part in the worship life of Hopwood Christian Church (Milligan College, Tennessee).

WORKS CITED

- Bacon, Leonard. "Critique of Pure Diabolism." Rev. of *The Screwtape Letters* by C.S. Lewis. *Saturday Review of Literature*. April 17, 1943:20.

- Gibson, Evan K. *C.S. Lewis: Spinner of Tales*. Grand Rapids, Michigan: Eerdmans, 1980.

- Green, Roger Lancelyn and Hooper, Walter. *C.S. Lewis: A Biography*. London: Souvenir Press, 1988.

- Holmer, Paul L. *C.S. Lewis: The Shape of His Faith and Thought*. New York: Harper and Row, 1976.

- Lewis, C.S. *The Screwtape Letters*. New York: Macmillan, 1961.

- _____. "Screwtape Proposes a Toast." *The Screwtape Letters.* New York: Macmillan, 1961 (151-172).

- Mencken, H.L. and Nathan, George Jean. "Clinical Notes." *American Mercury.* January 1925:59. Quoted in Perry, Ralph Barton. *Puritanism and Democracy.* New York: Harper and Row, 1944.

- Milton, John. *Paradise Lost. The Norton Anthology of English Literature.* Ed. M.H. Abrams *et. al.* Sixth edition. Vol. 1:1474-1610. New York: Norton, 1993.

- Sayer, George. *Jack: A Life of C.S. Lewis.* Second edition. Wheaton, Illinois: Crossway Books, 1994.

- Wilson, A.N. *C.S. Lewis: A Biography.* New York: Norton, 1990.

C.S. Lewis and the Holy Spirit

By Kathryn Lindskoog

C.S. Lewis was embarrassed by the phenomenon of speaking in tongues; but he once preached an entire sermon about the subject. According to the June 2, 1944 issue of *The Daily Telegraph*, "in the middle of the sermon Mr. Lewis, under stress of emotion, stopped, saying 'I'm sorry,' and left the pulpit. ... After a hymn was sung, Mr. Lewis returned and finished his sermon ... on a deeply moving note."[1] That sermon exists to this day in the essay "Transposition" in *Screwtape Proposes a Toast and other pieces*.[2]

Lewis believed in angels and demons and a thoroughly supernatural reality. He believed in mystical experience. I suspect that if he had lived ten years longer he might have welcomed the charismatic movement that was coming to the Anglican Church.

So it was that on Sunday, May 28, 1944, Lewis found himself preaching his memorable Pentecost Sunday sermon at Mansfield College Chapel in Oxford. He admitted at the start that *glossolalia*, speaking in tongues, was a subject that was a problem to him. (It would have been a problem for his listeners also.) But since it is part of the story of Pentecost, and since St. Paul said he spoke with tongues more than anyone else, Lewis felt he should deal with the subject.

To begin with, Lewis assumed that some cases of speaking in unknown tongues are just expressions of nervous excitement. But that doesn't mean that tongues can't ever be the work of the Holy Spirit. If some cases of speaking in tongues are this-worldly, Lewis insisted, it does not follow that other cases aren't genuinely spiritual.

The English that some saints use to talk about God sounds much like the expressions that human lovers use, but that does not mean that the saints are only fooling themselves about spiritual love. All spiritual things as we know them resemble parts of ordinary physical life. In fact, real human love would look like some kind of lust to humans who have never felt any love. Things can be far above the things that they resemble.

Furthermore, some of our physical sensations serve for two or more kinds of events. Lewis himself noticed that gorgeous music and bad news both caused the same odd feeling in his chest. He loved the feeling when it was part of his pleasure and hated it when it was part of his misery. The fact is that we have far more emotions than the physical responses to go with them. So our physical responses are multi-purpose. (Readers can think of their own examples. A person may weep with sorrow or with joy or from peeling onions; laugh with anger or with delight or from being tickled; tremble with terror or with ecstasy or from a chilly breeze.)

Our spiritual life manifests itself through our physical life. Speaking in tongues as a holy activity might sound just like meaningless gibberish to an outsider, but those on the inside know the difference. Spiritual things must be spiritually understood. There will always be people who say that religion is nothing but psychological need, justice nothing but self-protection, love nothing but lust, and thought nothing but twitching of the grey matter in the brain. (Since Lewis's time this reductionism has been labeled "nothing-buttery.") People who think this way are like a dog that looks at the pointing finger instead of at what the finger is pointing at. They miss the meaning of everything.

At the end of his sermon, Lewis looked ahead to the resurrection of the body. Perhaps when the Holy Spirit causes Christians to speak in tongues, that is a tiny sample of what lies ahead for us. Lewis supposed that in our resurrected bodies there will be far fuller experiences of God Himself. We probably won't have new senses, but our present senses will be flooded by God in ways we cannot now imagine.

Lewis not only believed in the supernatural gift of tongues, but he also believed in the reality of miracles; he twice preached sermons in London on that topic. Eventually he wrote an entire book called *Miracles: A Preliminary Study*,[3] ending with an afterthought: if we were heroic missionaries, apostles or martyrs, we would be apt to see miracles. Miracles and martyrdoms, he warned, tend to cluster in certain dangerous areas of history.

Later, Lewis witnessed the apparently miraculous healing of his wife's cancer after he called in a friend to pray for her when she was on her deathbed early in 1957. Their brief marriage after her healing was the happiest part of both their lives. Then she died in 1960.

Lewis published one of his last books, *The Four Loves*,[4] in 1960. At the end of the book he spoke of bereavement. It is no good seeking earthly comfort for our losses, he said. In the long run there is no earthly comfort. But heaven offers us heavenly comfort. What we loved in people here, we will find in Him. "By loving Him more than them we shall love them more than we now do."[5] In the meantime, we must try to believe what we cannot feel in our bereavement, that God is our true Beloved.

But God sometimes awakens in man, towards Himself, a supernatural Love. (Is this not a gift of the Holy Spirit?) Of all gifts this one is the most to be desired; this is the centre of all human and angelic life. Lewis thought that he had tasted this heavenly love for God, but just a little. "But for news of the fully waking world you must go to my betters," he said.[6] Three years later he went to "the fully waking world" himself. There, no doubt, he is flooded by God in ways we cannot now imagine.

Kathryn Lindskoog (1934-2003)

Kathryn Lindskoog was born in Petaluma, California. She received her B.A., magna cum laude, at the University of Redlands in 1956. She also received an academic scholarship to a University of London summer school in 1956. She received her M.A., magna cum laude, at California State University at Long Beach in 1957. Her thesis was entitled "The Lion of Judah in Never-Never Land." She took a Chapman University academic credit tour of Europe and Russia in 1960.

C.S. Lewis's 1957 handwritten response to Lindskoog's thesis included the following: "you know my work better than anyone else I've met: certainly better than I do myself."

She was the author of many books, including *C.S. Lewis: Mere Christian* (Harold Shaw Publishers, third edition 1987), *The Lion of Judah in Never-Never Land: God, Man and Nature in C.S. Lewis's Narnia Tales* (William B. Eerdmans Publishing Company, 1973),*Up From Eden* (David C. Cook Publishing Company, 1976), *The C.S. Lewis Hoax* (Multnomah, 1988), *Creative Writing For People Who Can't Not Write* (Zondervan Publishing House, 1989), *Fakes, Frauds and Other Malarkey: 301 Amazing Stories and How Not to be Fooled* (Zondervan Publishing House, 1993), and *Finding the Landlord: A Guidebook to C.S. Lewis's Pilgrim's Regress* (Cornerstone Press, 1995). She edited *The Lewis Legacy: Newsletter of the C.S. Lewis Foundation For Truth in Publishing* (1989-2003).

END NOTES

1. *The Daily Telegraph*, June 2, 1944.

2. C.S. Lewis, *Screwtape Proposes a Toast and other pieces* (Great Britain: Fount Paperbacks, 1977), p. 75-93.

3. C.S. Lewis, *Miracles: A preliminary Study* (Great Britain: Fontana Books, 1960).

4. C.S. Lewis, *The Four Loves* (Great Britain: Fount Paperbacks, 1977).

5. *Ibid.*, p. 127.

6. *Ibid.*, p. 128.

FRIGHTENED BY UNICORNS:
THE NARRATOR OF *THE GREAT DIVORCE*

By George Musacchio

Although it has been fifty years since C.S. Lewis first published *The Great Divorce: A Dream* in book form (1945), the brief adult fantasy is still timely in its spiritual and social themes. Those who have read it will recall that it is the story of an assortment of souls who travel by flying bus from a "grey town" (17) to the outskirts of Heaven. There the ghostly passengers meet some Solid People in a world so solid that the ghosts cannot bend the grass blades as they walk. The solid saints invite them to stay and grow solid themselves, but most choose to return to their dreary life below.

Readers may even recall their favourite characters: perhaps the apostate bishop who must return to Hell in time to read his paper at the theological society; or the glorious Sarah Smith of Golders Green; or the man with the lizard on his shoulder. But I want to focus on the narrator himself, who undergoes a major, and easily overlooked, change in the course of his Dantesque journey.

Like Dante, Lewis narrates the story in the first person, as if he himself had experienced the journey that turns out at the end to be a dream. Of course we do not take him literally, as if he were recounting an actual dream. But for the sake of simplicity I will call the narrator Lewis as we trace this central character's climactic change.

Once the bus lands (ch. 3), Lewis becomes a fairly detached observer, watching the ghosts encounter their solid environment and react to the Solid People. But in chapter 7 he experiences a downward turn that leaves him depressed and miserable. Will it prove to be the darkness before his dawn? Before we answer that, let us observe the cause of his misery.

His depression comes from his conversation with a tall, "hard-bitten" ghost from Hell (53), a cynic who has nothing good to say about their beautiful (but very solid) surroundings on the outskirts of Heaven. "You don't think of staying?" asks Lewis. That would be impossible, the ghost assures him. "You can't eat the fruit and you can't drink the water and it takes you all your time to walk on the grass. A human being couldn't live here" (54).

"There seems to be some idea that if one stays here one would get—well, solider—grow acclimatized," says Lewis (55). But again the Hard-Bitten Ghost is cynical: it's all lies, propaganda from the Management, "the same old Ring" that runs things here and in Hell (55). What's more, it will probably rain soon in this solid world where "every raindrop will make a hole in you, like a machine-gun bullet" (57). No wonder our narrator says, "A great depression had come over me" (57).

At the end of chapter 7, the cynic leaves. Chapter 8 begins: "I sat still on a stone by the river's side feeling as miserable as I ever felt in my life. Hitherto it had not occurred to me to doubt the intentions of the Solid People, nor to question the essential goodness of their country even if it were a country which I could not long inhabit" (58). Affected by the ghost's cynicism, Lewis ponders: "How if [the Solid People] had never meant to do us good at all? How if this whole trip were allowed the Ghosts merely to mock them?" (58). His questions hit at the heart of the book, the matter of choice: Heaven or Hell. Can the ghosts choose to stay in this solid country? Since the arrival of the bus in chapter 3, the narrator has seen no one decide to try. "If only I could find a trace of evidence that it was really possible for a Ghost to stay—that the choice were not only a cruel comedy— I would not go back" (59).

Walking on, he comes to a clearing and watches a ghost encounter a Solid Person, as he had watched others throughout chapters 3-6. But this time the result will be different.

The ghost is a woman experiencing shame. Acutely aware that her appearance reveals all too well her inner emptiness, she is too ashamed to be seen, much less allow the solid spirit to help her progress in the right direction. She has the proper awareness of her spiritual poverty but is making the improper response (for a fruitful response, see Len's story recounted in ch. 3). The Solid Person explains that she must "drink the cup [of shame] to the bottom" and then will find it nourishing (61-62).

"You really mean?" begins the ghost, for a moment entertaining the idea that she can be saved, can choose to stay there and become solid—the seeming impossibility of which has depressed the narrator.

Lewis says, "My suspense was strained up to the height. I felt that my own destiny hung on her reply" (62). If she accepts the offer and goes with the Spirit, then the good news is true, and Lewis too will choose to stay.

But she does not. Her mind firmly fixed on herself, impoverished though she recognizes that self to be, she rejects the Spirit's offer.

"'Then only one expedient remains,' said the Spirit, and to my great surprise he set a horn to his lips and blew" (62). Lewis hears "the thudding of hoofs" drawing near, "and soon so near that I began to look about for some place of safety. Before I had found one the danger was all about us. A herd of unicorns came thundering through the glades" (62-63).

Both the narrator and the ghost are frightened by these huge creatures tossing their horns as in battle. "I heard the Ghost scream, and I think it made a bolt away from the bushes...perhaps towards the Spirit, but I don't know. For my own nerve failed and I fled" (63; ellipsis in original).

Why does the Spirit call the unicorns? What is the nature of this one remaining "expedient"? Later Lewis learns that it was calculated to frighten the woman into salvation; "not that fear itself could make her less a Ghost, but if it took her mind a moment off herself, there might, in that moment, be a chance" (76). Apparently, fear has its place in the divine arsenal.

But we notice that the narrator was also frightened by the unicorns—the depressed narrator who felt as if his destiny hung with the woman's. Does the fright do him any good?

Yes, for as he "fled, not heeding, for the moment, the horrible going underfoot, and not once daring to pause" (63), he runs right into the presence of George MacDonald (64), a Solid Person who will guide him the rest of his journey. As Beatrice led Dante to Heaven, MacDonald leads Lewis through the outskirts of Heaven, interpreting for him the encounters between ghosts and Solid People, explaining the issues of free will, power, and love at work before his eyes.

Chapter 9, then, when the narrator meets MacDonald, is a major turning point for "Lewis" in the story. The miserable traveller, on the point of despair, has been frightened into finding just the helper he needs. From here on he is no longer the simple observer of the early chapters. What he sees becomes rich with meaning, thanks to MacDonald. And subsequently what we readers see becomes richer, as if Lewis the author himself has finally found his way among his materials. Chapters 10-11 show improper loves in action; chapter 12 gives us Sarah Smith, the Lady of Proper Love, whose story goes on into chapter 13 as her husband the dwarf-ghost struggles against the joy she offers him; and chapters 13-14 give us rich symbols of the mysteries of time, eternity, free will, and providence, coming to the denouement of our narrator awakening from his dream with a crash.

The frightful unicorns, a pleasure to read about, turn out to be more than an author's vivid, imaginative episode meant to enliven the story. In addition, as we note that they frighten the narrator into the presence of George MacDonald, who banishes his doubts and misery, so we may hope that they scare the shame-ridden ghost out of herself and into the arms of the Solid Person, who stands ready to lead her further up and further into Heaven. Thus engaged in our reading of *The Great Divorce*, we demonstrate its enduring timeliness for spiritual nourishment fifty years after its first publication in book form.

GEORGE MUSACCHIO

George Musacchio is a native Kentuckian who spent many years in California. For twenty-five years he taught English at what is now California Baptist University, his undergraduate alma mater. His M.A. and Ph.D. degrees in English are from the University of California, Riverside. From 1977 through 1980 he edited the *Lamp-Post*, the journal of the Southern California C.S. Lewis Society, and he is currently a contributing editor of that literary review.

He has been a Visiting Professor at Baylor University, Calvin College, and Golden Gate Baptist Theological Seminary. In the summer of 1988 he attended part of the first C.S. Lewis Summer Institute in Oxford, England. And as of 2005 he has attended each subsequent, usually triennial, Summer Institute held by the C.S. Lewis Foundation of Redlands, California.

In 1990 he moved to Texas to become Professor of English and the first holder of the Frank W. Mayborn Chair of Arts and Sciences at the University of Mary Hardin-Baylor. He retired at the end of May 2004 and now holds the honourary title of Vann Research Professor at the University.

Dr. Musacchio has presented papers on literary topics at conferences from California to Oxford. He has published dozens of articles and book reviews, many of them concerning C.S. Lewis. His two books are *Milton's Adam and Eve* (1991) and *C.S. Lewis, Man and Writer: Essays and Reviews* (1994, available through Amazon.com's Marketplace).

WORK CITED

- C.S. Lewis, *The Great Divorce*. New York: Macmillan, 1963.

TRAINED HABIT:
THE SPIRITUALITY OF C.S. LEWIS

By Nancy-Lou Patterson

"If we were perfected, prayer would not be a duty, it would be a delight."

C.S. Lewis, *Letters to Malcolm: Chiefly On Prayer*[1]

Although his conversion and subsequent role as a Christian apologist and writer of Christian fantasy are extremely well known, C.S. Lewis's spirituality is not much discussed and not well understood. This is the case for two reasons. First, one's spirituality is a very private matter, or ought to be. Jesus told His followers to go into their closets when they undertook to pray, and followed His own teaching, not least at Gethsemane, even though His visits to both Temple and Synagogue tended to be strikingly public. Secondly, Lewis consistently hid his personal life in plain sight, disguised in a variety of forms, some supposedly fictional and some supposedly autobiographical.

James Como has pointed out that *Surprised by Joy: The Shape of My Early Life, Reflections on the Psalms, Letters to Malcolm: Chiefly on Prayer*, and even *A Grief Observed* "all show signs of formal, or generic distortion—even contrivance, in the latter two—for rhetorical purposes" (Como, 1993, p. 6-7). Indeed, George Musacchio has argued that *A Grief Observed* should be read "as a fictional journal intended to help its readers through actual crises of grief and faith" (Musacchio, 1994, p. 110). Both writers are right, for the reasons I have already given. Lewis always hid, or rather, disguised, his personal life. His first autobiographical work, *The Pilgrim's Regress: An Allegorical Apology for Christianity, Reason and Romanticism*, was based upon the story of his conversion, but told in the full armour of allegory. Even in his openly autobiographical *Surprised by Joy*, he entirely excluded his relationship with Mrs. Janie Moore, and hence, nearly all of his adult private life. He published *A Grief Observed*—certainly, directly related to his wife, Joy Davidman's, death—anonymously.

In the same manner, for the same reason—a desire for privacy even while addressing his most intimate concerns—*Letters to Malcolm: Chiefly on Prayer*, presented in fictional terms as a series of letters from an unnamed writer to the equally fictional Malcolm, contains many elements that are demonstrably autobiographical. Happily for us, it gives a clear picture of his spirituality in its lived form. That is, it accords in many ways with what not only Lewis, but other writers who knew him well, said about his customary practice as regards private prayer and public worship. Simply put, the anonymous letter-writer has the same habits as the book's author.

Furthermore, the opinions expressed by that letter-writer about these customary activities are, as can be shown by comparisons to others of his writings, including personal letters, Lewis's as well, especially in matters that really *matter*. As a most telling example, I offer the following. When the letter-writer tells Malcolm, "I believe in Purgatory" (139) he expresses Lewis's own opinion, already given in a variety of places. It would be hard to imagine any other author writing in Lewis's most characteristic and inimitable manner,

> Our souls *demand* Purgatory, don't they? Would it not break the heart if God said to us, "it is true, my son, that...your rags drip with mud...but we are charitable here...enter into the joy?" Should we not reply, "with submission, Sir, and if there is no objection, I'd *rather* be cleaned first. (140)

As regards the fictional friendship between the correspondents, this too shows a distinctly autobiographical flavour, with neither "..."

(as he is styled in the book) nor "Malcolm" matching the description of them attributed to Lewis by his biographers Roger Lancelyn Green and Walter Hooper, who say that according to him, "the reader is merely being allowed to listen to two very ordinary laymen" and that "the author [that is, the supposed author of the letters] does *not* claim to be teaching" (Green and Hooper, 1974, p. 233). In fact, this work demands a relatively high level of sophistication in us as well as in Malcolm. It is full of references to works of literature as well as of theological debate both contemporary (circa 1964) and into the remote past. On the first page he uses the Latin term *agendum*, cites the *Republic*, and refers to "liturgiology" (11). Before the end of this chapter he has referred to "the Grail" (13), mentioned "the gradual change of spelling in successive editions of Shakespeare" (15), quoted in Psalm 24, which contains the phrase "Be ye lift up," and mentions "what you say about Rose Macula's letters" (17). These may be "ordinary laymen" in Oxford or Cambridge (or, of course, in other places where well-educated people gather), but it is a long way from these imaginary correspondents to the radio audience presupposed by, say, the contents of *Mere Christianity*, not to say most television viewers of today. I don't mean to say that these matters cannot be made plain to most listeners; Lewis had a great gift for that, and it is probably his most educated listeners who need to hear this message most. Even so, the conversation between Lewis's letter-writer and Malcolm strongly suggests, at the very least, the circle of Lewis's actual friends, the Inklings, with one very notable and autobiographical exception, the mention of Malcolm's "literary wife" (22), Betty, who in her ability to get to the heart of a matter, resembles Lewis's own literary wife, Joy. When the writer says "You and I have both known happy marriage. But how different our wives were from the imaginary mistresses of our adolescent dreams! So much less exquisitely adapted to all our wishes; and for that reason (among others) so incomparably better" (102), who can doubt that Lewis could only have written this after, rather than before, his actual marriage?

This question has bearing upon the book's history. Begun in 1952 (Green and Hooper, p. 232), the work was completed in the last year of Lewis's life. He wrote on April 22, 1963 (seven months before he died): "I've finished a book on Prayer. Don't know if it is any good" (Lewis, 1967, p. 113). It seems to me that Lewis discovered his book's method by, first, an adult's lifetime of prayer and worship, and second, by having lived to experience in full the kind of life he gives to his imaginary letter-writer, culminating in the bereavement which he had chosen to describe in quasi-fictional form in A *Grief Observed*.

Several authors have attempted to characterize *Letters to Malcolm*. Alan Bede Griffiths, OSB, says of Lewis, "he had a profound kind of mystical intuition...and there are times, especially in the *Letters to Malcolm*, when he comes near to a genuine mystical insight" (p. 23). Appropriately, then, George Sayer regarded *Letters to Malcolm* as "a devotional book," characterizing it as "a series of reflections on prayer" (1988, p. 187). In both ways—as a devotional book which comes near to genuine mystical insight, this slim volume much resembles the many superb little books on spirituality by Evelyn Underhill, based in her case upon addresses given at retreats. Like them, it can be read a chapter (or less) at a time, in a meditative way, as well as all the way through at one go. I confess that when I read it the first time, having acquired it during Holy Week 1964, I found it disappointing. Re-reading it at the age of 65, having approximately matched its author in longevity if not in spiritual achievement, I found that it went straight to the heart, and that experience has resulted in the present essay.

PRAYER

The secret of Lewis's spirituality lies, as my title says, in the "trained habit—*habito dell' arte*" (13). Malcolm's correspondent applies this term to "the art of worship," and Lewis clearly attempted to apply it to both public worship and private prayer, acts not really very far apart in an actively lived spiritual life. Lewis's spirituality, most particularly, sets an example we all hope for, one attainable to the ordinary Christian. Here, he met, with a long consistency, the basic requirements of "mere Christianity": regular, daily prayer—"pray without ceasing" (1 Thessalonians 5:17)—and regular, consistent attendance at public worship— "not forsaking the assembling of ourselves together" (Hebrews 10:25)—both fundamental practices based very firmly upon Scripture and set forth in *The Book of Common Prayer*. This last is a matter of significance, since Owen Barfield has stated that "the impression I get from his writings is that he just accepts Christian doctrine as developed by, particularly, the Anglican Church, which of course until a few years ago was agreed on the matter. He accepts it as final revelation...or as final interpretation of final revelation" (1989, p. 138).

People who knew Lewis well attest that he prayed daily. George Sayer describes a visit by Lewis in 1951. About "five in the evening," he recalls, "if there was not already one in his room, he would then ask for a Bible 'in any translation' and say his prayers. He found this the best time of day for them" (1988, p. 207). Again, Sayer reports, in an essay entitled "Jack On Holiday," that "he liked to arrive very early at Oxford station, to walk up and down the platform saying his prayers" (1979, p. 203). And yet again, "Back home [from a day of walking] Jack would wash all over in his bedroom ... read in the Bible ... and say his prayers. He found this the best time of day for religious devotions" (1979, p. 204-205).

Lewis himself has attested to his custom of prayer repeatedly in the letters included in *Letters To An American Lady*. "Of course I have been praying for you daily, as always," he wrote on November 6, 1953 (Lewis, 1967, p. 21); "You may be very sure of my continued ... prayers" (Lewis, 1967, p. 53); "I shall pray for you whenever I wake in the night" (Lewis, 1967, p. 55); "Of course you are always in my prayers" (Lewis, 1967, p. 84); and "Thank you for all your kind prayers. You have mine daily" (Lewis, 1967, p. 10). "Daily," "continued," "always," "whenever I wake in the night": these are the watch-words of the Christian attuned to the command to "pray without ceasing."

Exactly this element of habitual prayer can be seen in *Letters to Malcolm*. Lewis is clearly like his imaginary letter-writer, who tells Malcolm that he prays "sitting in a crowded train" (28) and on "a bench in the park" (28), "with a concentrated mind and a sitting body" (30). And he remarks, surely from personal experience, that "those who do not turn to God in petty trials have no *habit* [his emphasis] or such resort to help them when the great trials come" (36-37).

But there is more to Lewis's prayer than its regular, consistent usage. What *form* does his prayer take? Here *Letters to Malcolm* is especially useful, defining the relationship established in prayer: "The relationship between God and [humankind]...is more private and intimate than any possible relation between two fellow creatures" (23). One who prays becomes, in Lewis's (or his imaginary writer's) astonishing words, "the fellow-worker, the companion, or (dare we say?) the colleague of God" (84). In this situation, we "put ourselves ... on a personal footing with God," and "He, descending, becomes a Person to us" (33).

It is striking, then, to learn that (at least in the case of Malcolm's imaginary correspondent, and, I suggest, in the life of C.S. Lewis) "for many years after my conversion I never used any ready-made forms except the Lord's Prayer" (20). How did he manage to do this? Not, apparently, by repeating it endlessly as one does the Jesus Prayer, or in regular settings, as one does in praying the Rosary. The answer to this question concerning an apparently very simple style of prayer proves to be extraordinarily significant.

In discussing the matter, Lewis refers to "'my festooning'—the private overtones I give to certain petitions" (38). These petitions are those of the Lord's Prayer, the prayer that Jesus taught to those who asked Him, "Lord, teach us to pray" (Luke 11:1). These festoons, apparently, developed as a kind of meditation, "added gradually" (39) as the author/writer at prayer sought for deeper and greater understanding; trying as Paul says in 1 Corinthians 14:15, to "pray with the understanding also." Indeed, the details as given in *Letters to Malcolm* comprise an illuminating meditation upon the meaning of that matchless and inexhaustible prayer.

But what does Lewis (and I do mean Lewis) *mean* by the word "festoon"? He uses it not only for the Lord's Prayer but for "the whole previous history of the real universe—which is not itself an 'instance' of anything," and says that this "real universe" is "therefore always festooned with those particularities which science for her own purposes quite rightly discounts" (58). Each festoon, then, whether added through meditation to the Lord's Prayer, or occurring in the "real universe" we all share, represents a particularity rather than a generality. For Lewis, the "festoons" he drapes upon the structure of the Lord's Prayer are both the intellectual elaborations and interpretations of a particular scholar and the applications of its petitions to the particularities of that scholar's daily life. For scholar, read person, man, woman, child or what you will.

As always with Lewis, this obvious interpretation is deepened by an examination of the specific words—or in this case, word—"festoon"—which he has chosen to express his ideas. *Webster's Collegiate Dictionary* derives "festoon" from *festa* (feast). Used as a noun, the word means "a garland or wreath hanging in a curve, used in decoration for festivals." Used as a verb, it means to "adorn ... with festoons."[2] Are Lewis's meditations upon the Lord's Prayer then a form of festive decoration, and are his petitions intended to adorn? At the least, one can say so. The word "decoration" itself is related to "decorum" with its overtones of seemliness and propriety, not in our usual sense of outward show but in the much faded sense of doing what is really and indeed right and proper.

The word "festoon," especially in its variant, "garland," has a long and profoundly significant history, of which Lewis is unlikely to have been ignorant. In twentieth-century symbolism, the garland is seen as "the token bonds or connection" (Cirlot, 1962, p. 110) as in the saying cited from Eliphas Levi (1920): "Everything in the universe is likely to have been made, an image of the fleeting, the ephemeral, as well as of the linkage between life and death." The festoon or garland can be seen, even in such simplified terms, as representing a link between a single consciousness (read "soul") and the divine, human life being indeed fleeting and ever close to death, and to all that may lie beyond.

For the historical anthropologist, the garland or festoon was used for guests at festive entertainments in ancient Egypt (Goody, 1993, p. 39) and subsequently was incorporated into the cultures of Greece and Rome (with the addition, from the Near East, of the rose as a floral component), recurring in Medieval and Renaissance Europe and consequently still used in the twentieth century where ornament is required. At the simplest, the fixing of such elements as the festoon or garland into "schematic" motifs (Goody, 1993, p. 57) makes them available as stock or habitual forms, useful for "framing, filling, and linking" in decoration, while retaining their aspect of "prestige" (Goody, 1993, p. 52). One recalls that Lewis recommended "stock responses" as a powerful armour in situations of temptation, another example of his idea of the "trained habit."

Interestingly, while garlands were used in ancient Greece for "joyful" occasions (Goody, 1993, p. 86) such as weddings or while offering a gift to a divinity (the old meaning of the word "sacrifice"), in ancient Rome, garlands came to be associated also with funerals. In Pompeii, they were "painted on the walls of the shrine rooms" (Goody, 1993, p. 67) of family homes, dedicated to the household gods, as well as in rooms associated with banquets and drinking, when the sacred association of wine with Dionysus still lingered. Gradually, "the garland, including painted and sculpted ones," became "more significant than the offering" (Goody, 1993, p. 70); in fact they *became* the offering in some cases. Lewis, then, makes his little festoons, his meditations and intercessions, into *offerings*, as part of his prayers, hanging them upon the branches of his Lord's own great and universal prayer.

As one might suspect, a motif so deeply associated with "pagan" life did not pass unscathed through the examination of the early church, but it was the crown of flowers, as opposed to the crown of thorns, rather than "flowers or garlands in themselves" (Goody, 1993, p. 76) that caught the attention of the early writers. In specific cases, where garlands were used as offerings to pre-Christian divinities, this use was of course anathema to Christians. On the other hand, "Early Christians had used the...garland as designs in their tombs and catacombs" (Goody, 1993, p. 84), and long after aboriginal Europe had been Christianized, the motif of the garland has continued to exist, even into the Postmodern period, where architects have retained (revived) it in its role as a surviving element of Classical ornament.

It is perfectly likely that this long historical sequence was in play in Lewis's choice of the word "festoon"; not only was he a specialist in the literature of the Medieval and Renaissance periods, but he had personally experienced the custom, in Anglican churches, of festooning the parish church with garlands, particularly at Harvest Home (Thanksgiving) and Christmas. The custom had survived the predations of the Puritans during the Civil War and had returned, along with Christmas itself, after the Restoration. Readers of Lewis's friend Dorothy L. Sayers will remember that in *The Nine Tailors*. Lord Peter Wimsey had, during a very rainy Christmas season, "assisted Mrs. Venables [the Rector's wife] to tie wet branches of holly and ivy to the font" (Sayers, 1975, p. 332).

Beyond the Lord's Prayer, Lewis's prayer obviously included reading the Bible, and clearly he read it daily. We know that he always re-read the books he had enjoyed; apparently this book of all books is the one he re-read the most, every day, in fact. With others of his books, as he wrote to Arthur Greeves, he would treat them "as a sort of hobby" (Lewis, 1979, p. 438), making lists of key words and quotations on the flyleaves, drawing maps and charts and outlines. Did he do this with the Bible? Mentally, at least, he must have done, for his writing is rich in allusions to and inclusions of passages from the Bible. Careful and regular Bible reading, then, formed a central feature of his prayers. One cannot be surprised at this. The daily prayers in *The Book of Common Prayer*, based upon the monastic hours and derived ultimately from the customs of the Synagogue, include Scripture, the Psalms (Lewis wrote a book on them; he obviously knew many of them by heart and had meditated long and deeply upon them), and the Lord's Prayer, which appears twice both in Matins and Evensong.

I would suggest that Lewis's combination of intercession—"I have been praying for you daily"—and meditation—"my festooning"—provides a plan for prayer that every Christian can follow, especially when accompanied, as it was in Lewis's case, by daily Bible reading. Our daily lives can provide the content for such prayers, through which by day and by night we can offer up not only ourselves but all that we know and love.

THE SACRAMENT

In *Letters to Malcolm*, Lewis offers what may be his most important dictum: "We have no non-religious activities" (46). He expresses this profound idea twice, in slightly differing form, thus: "all ground is holy and every bush (could we but perceive it) a burning bush" (100), and again, "Here is the holy ground; the bush is burning now" (109). Both time and space offer the moment of contact between humankind and God, and both are in action in this encounter.

We notice that in this situation, when in the here and now God and humanity meet, Lewis turns, as in his great fantasies, to the language of wonder; indeed, the biblical account of the Burning Bush employs an image of absolute potency. And here the intellect stumbles as the analogical level of consciousness surpasses and outruns it; Lewis says that in the Eucharist, "the veil between the worlds, nowhere else (to me) so opaque to the intellect, is nowhere else so thin and permeable to divine operation" (133).

His imaginary writer says in one place, "my ideas about the sacrament would probably be called 'magical' by a good many modern theologians" (18), and in another place he calls the Eucharist the centre of "the magical element in Christianity," indeed, "as magical" as "the existence of God as *causa sui*" (135), that is, self-caused.

"Magic" in this context refers to the role of the Sacrament as being both physical and spiritual, and hence a scandal to those who would like it to be either one or the other. In one of his letters, Lewis had written, "I think all that extreme refinement and that spirituality which takes the form of despising matter, is very like Pythagoras and Plato and Marcus Aurelius. Poor dears: they don't know about the Sacraments nor the resurrection of the body" (Lewis, 1967, p. 57). That is, they don't know about the Incarnation and all its consequences. It was upon this point that the Gnostic elements in Christianity foundered.

Lewis himself did not always possess this knowledge—"the Sacraments nor the resurrection of the body." His conversion occurred during the period of 1926-31, by a process of gradual illumination; that is, "from 1926, the year *Dymer* was published, when he began to believe in a nebulous power outside himself, to 1931, when he became a believer in Christ" (Sayer, 1988, p. 129). As a result of this conversion, he became "a practicing Christian," a member of the Church of England, and "he received Communion for the first time since boyhood on Christmas day at the church in Headington, where he would be buried thirty-two years later" (Sayer, 1988, p. 135). During those years his custom regarding the actual acceptance of the Euchanstic elements (that is, actually receiving bread and wine during the ceremony) gradually changed. He began by receiving Communion "on...Christmas and Easter," but soon took up "Communion once a month" (Sayer, 1988, p. 135). George Sayer observed this usage "when he stayed with me at Malvern in the early 1950s," adding that during "the last fifteen or so years of his life, I think he normally received Communion every week" (Sayer, 1988, p. 135).

Owen Barfield, who obviously read *Letters to Malcolm* as autobiographical, once said, "Lewis confesses that in Holy Communion he hasn't the faintest idea of what is happening," but when asked "You mean he does it because he ought?" he replied, "Well, I wouldn't put it that way, because it certainly meant a lot to him" (Barfield, 1989, p. 149). In light of this, we can consider Alan Bede Griffith's statement that Lewis "was later to acquire a deep reverence for and understanding of the mystery of the Eucharist" (1979, p. 20). And on the same basis we can note that an observer who knew Lewis at Cambridge wrote, "It seems needless to say that the chapel was the centre of his life in college. He daily attended … matins at 8:00 o'clock." Matins (Morning Prayer) is not the Eucharist, but this observer adds that Lewis's regime of daily worship included not only "early rising" and "chapel" but "Communion at least once a week" (Como, 1979, p. 103).

Speaking for himself, Lewis wrote to his American correspondent: "Yes, private communions (I shared many during Joy's last days) are extraordinarily moving. I am in danger of preferring them to those in church" (Lewis, 1967, p. 112). In danger, that is, of preferring to worship in a small group—himself, his wife, his priest—rather than in a public setting with a wider circle of participants and (he hated hymns) the ever-present distractions of common life. Christians are permitted to enjoy a range of associations, from the one suggested by the promise of Jesus: "For when two or three are gathered together in my name, there am I in the midst of them" (Matthew 18:20) to "Not forsaking the assembling of ourselves together" (Hebrews 10:25). We read in Acts 20:7 of the regular occasions "upon the first day of the week, when the disciples came together to break bread," and in Acts 2:42 of how "they continued steadfastly in the apostles' doctrine and fellowship, and in breaking of bread, and in prayers." Prayer by itself (let alone by oneself) is not enough; there must be bread broken as well, and it must be broken with others.

It is as a recent Canadian Anglican parish history puts it: "It has been in its insistence on the fact that God is both mediated and worshipped through the created order of 'matter' ... and not through a rejection of the world" (Ross, 1993, p. 514), that the Eucharist witness of Anglican worship has been made manifest, as it has by all Christians according to their own particular usages. Clearly, Lewis understood and lived "the essential connection between created order ('the world') and the worship of God expressed in the sacramental life of the Church" (Ross, 1993, p. 513).

The reason he refuses to state (or even more likely to reach a conclusion about or search for a precise definition of) what "happens" in the Eucharist is very simple. First, it (in its fullness) is never fully knowable to *anybody*; and second, much blood has been spilled in the past, literally, along with much ink, over the subject, and Lewis always avoided matters of inter-church and intra-church controversy. In this he was most particularly and characteristically Anglican, following the retort attributed to Queen Elizabeth I:

> His was the word that spake it,
> And what that word doth make it,
> That I believe and take it.

Bishop J.W.C. Wand explains that during the reign of Edward VI (Henry VIII's son and successor), the "main struggle in doctrinal reform was over the Presence of Christ in the Eucharist" (Ward, 1961, p. 18). Richard Hooker (1553-1600), a man of whom Lewis was an admirer, "seems to have adopted a teaching of the Real Presence" (Wand, 1961, p. 22). That is, a teaching regarding the question of whether Jesus was, or was not, really present in the Elements (Bread and Wine) of the Eucharist (and, if present, present in what way).

Along with the question of the Presence of Christ in the Eucharist, there was the equally vexed matter of "the doctrine of eucharist sacrifice" (Wilson, 1980, p. 340). That is, what exactly is meant by saying that the Eucharist is a sacrifice? A.G. Herbert, a contemporary of Lewis, spoke of the Eucharist "not merely as Sacrifice, not merely as Communion," but as Sacrifice consummated in Communion," adding, like the liturgical Revivalist he was, "communion of the people" is "the central act of worship every Sunday" (1935, p. 13). When this was written, such was by no means the case, and nor was it (or is it) everywhere or anywhere entirely the case even today among Anglicans, though it is far, far more common than it used to be. Lewis's gradually changing custom, from receiving Communion twice a year to receiving it once a week, accords, even so, with changes wrought over his lifetime as well, presumably, as by changes in his chosen practice.

If we want to know what Lewis understood about the two doctrinal matters—the Eucharist as Sacrifice or Remembrance, and Christ as present in or symbolized by the Eucharist—it is useful to consult *The Book of Common Prayer*. Article XXVIII of "The Articles of Religion" states that "to such as rightly, worthily, and with faith, receive the same, the Bread which we break is a partaking of the Body of Christ; and likewise the Cup of Blessing is a partaking of the Blood of Christ." And for those who may wish to enquire further, there is the following exchange in the Catechism:

> Q. What is the outward part or sign of the Lord's Supper?
>
> A. Bread and Wine, which the Lord hath commanded to be received.
>
> Q. What is the inward part, or thing signified?
>
> A. The Body and Blood of Christ, which are verily and indeed taken and received by the faithful in the Lord's Supper.
>
> Q. What are the benefits thereof we are partakers thereby?
>
> A. The strengthening and refreshing of our soul by the Body and Blood of Christ, as our bodies are by the Bread and Wine.

To Lewis, surely, that all seemed clear and straightforward enough: apparent opposition such as Body and Soul, outward sign and thing signified, Bread and Body, Cup and Blood, are shown to be mutually defining realities, so simple as to be acceptable without further enquiry, and so complex as to defy all attempts to achieve an exhaustive understanding.

Lewis, who "always affected ... to be a plain, honest man" (Como, 1979, p. 12), makes his alter ego, the correspondent of *Letters to Malcolm*, say "The truth is, I haven't any language weak enough to depict the weakness of my spiritual life" (109). We should consider the truth of this veiled self-evaluation in the light of the evidence, given above, of a man who "was as disciplined in his religion, especially his prayers, as he was in everything else" (Como, 1979, p. 103), a man who has been called (after the site of his final conversion), "St. Clive of Whipsnade" (Martin, 1993, p. 7). When we hear Lewis's apparent disclaimers, we should be reminded of what he wrote about the Holy Spirit in *Mere Christianity*: "Do not be worried or surprised if you find it (or Him) rather vaguer or more shadowy in your mind than the other two [Persons of the Holy Trinity].... In the Christian life you are not usually looking *at* Him: He is always acting through you" (Lewis, 1956, p. 136).

When Lewis called the Eucharist "opaque to the intellect" and spoke of "the weakness of [his] ... spiritual life," he made indeed and without affectation his common cause with "plain, honest" women and men, and we can be glad that he did! Owen Barfield says that "at a certain stage in [Lewis's] ... life he deliberately ceased to take any interest in himself as a kind of spiritual alumnus taking his moral finals" (1965, p. xvi). What began as a deliberate choice became at length "an ingrained and effortless habit of soul" (Barfield/Gibb, 1965, p. xvi).

A "habit of soul"—a willed simplicity—and a "trained habit": these are the keynotes of Lewis's spirituality. In his private prayers, he made an offering not only of his time, praying daily no matter where he found himself, and of his intercessory concerns, praying continuously for those he knew to be in spiritual or physical need (and his direct financial aid to great numbers of these people are amply documented, even though he, according to numerous witnesses, forgot about these acts of charity), but of his intellectual deliberations and meditative intuitions, festooning intercession and meditation alike upon the mighty edifice of the Lord's Prayer, as sacrificial garlands. In his public worship he left his privacy, to meet together not only with his personal friends and colleagues, but with whatever fellow Christians he found beside him in the pew, again in a regular, consistent, habitual way, not waiting for full understanding before undertaking the commandment to "take and eat" and to "drink this." This is neither ignorance nor weakness. In these acts of public worship, just as in his acts of private prayer, Lewis offered himself and all he cared for as sacrifice. If this is not weakness or ignorance, is it instead presumption, hubris, a wish to be seen to be spiritual? Is it an empty gesture, a rote repetition, a meaningless custom as many people seem to think these days?

In *The Book of Common Prayer*, in words repeated with every Eucharist, the worshippers declare, "and here we offer and present unto thee, O Lord, ourselves, our souls and bodies, to be a reasonable, holy, and lively [that is, 'living'] sacrifice unto Thee." This language is not weak, nor is it presumptuous. It calls for a total gift of one's intellect, one's spirituality, one's physicality, indeed, one's whole life, and nothing less. In this offering, day by day, and week by week, C.S. Lewis made it his trained habit to participate.

Sanctity, which is the goal of spirituality, arises from such habitual endeavour, from a trained regularity in encountering the mystery of the Incarnation. God gives us the grace to try, and takes our weakest efforts as if they were—say rather, because they are indeed—those of Christ Himself; of whose Body, C.S. Lewis was (and is), even as all Christians are called and intended to be, a part. Such spirituality is open to us all.

NANCY-LOU PATTERSON

Nancy-Lou Patterson is widely-known as a writer, artist, scholar, teacher, novelist and poet, whose educational and artistic career spans five decades. The daughter of academic parents, she was born in 1929 in Worcester, Massachusetts. She received her B.A. in Fine Arts from the University of Washington in 1951, afterwards working for two years as a

scientific illustrator at the University of Kansas and at the Smithsonian, then for nine years as a lecturer at Seattle University. In 1962 she moved to the Waterloo region, Ontario, with her husband, Dr. E. Palmer Patterson, who was to teach at the University of Waterloo. In addition to her position as Director of Art and Curator of the University's art gallery, in 1966 Professor Nancy-Lou Patterson taught the University of Waterloo's first Fine Arts course, and in 1968 she founded the Department of Fine Arts, twice serving as Department Chair. She became an Associate Professor in 1972 and full Professor in 1981.

As a scholar, Nancy-Lou is well known for her writings in the area of mythopoeic art and literature, with particular focus on the works of C.S. Lewis, J.R.R. Tolkien, George MacDonald, Charles Williams and Dorothy L. Sayers. She has written extensively on the art of Native Canadians (*Canadian Native Art: Arts and Crafts of Canadian Indians and Eskimos*). Her work includes both book and exhibition reviews, and exhibition catalogues. She has published both poetry and fiction, including *Apple Staff and Silver Crown*, *The Painted Hallway*, *Barricade Summer*, *The Tramp Room*, *The Quilted Grapevine*, *The Haunted Bed and Breakfast*, *The Spring House*, and *Snow Wall*. All of her stories include elements of fantasy in a variety of ways.

END NOTES

1 C.S. Lewis, *Letters to Malcolm: Chiefly on Prayer* (London), p. 147. Hereinafter cited in the text by page number only, as the primary source of this essay. Other sources, except for that given in endnote 2, are listed in "Works Cited," and cited in the text by author, date and page.

2 *Webster's Collegiate Dictionary* (Springfield, Massachusetts: G. and C. Merriam, 1947).

WORKS CITED

- Owen Barfield, *Owen Barfield on C.S. Lewis*. G.B. Tennyson (ed.). Middletown, Connecticut: Wesleyan University Press, 1989.

- J.E. Cirlot, *A Dictionary of Symbols*. New York: Philosophical Library, 1962.

- James Como, "The Centrality of Rhetoric to an Understanding of C.S. Lewis," *CSL: The Bulletin of the New York C.S. Lewis Society*, November 1993.

- Gibb, Jocelyn (ed.). *Light on C.S. Lewis*. New York: Harcourt Brace Jovanovich, 1965.

- Alan Bede Griffiths, OSB, "The Adventure of Faith," James T. Como (ed.), *C.S. Lewis at the Breakfast Table and Other Reminiscences*. New York: Macmillan, 1979.

- Jack Goody, *The Culture of Flowers*. Cambridge, England: The University of Cambridge Press, 1993.

- Roger Lancelyn Green and Walter Hooper, *C.S. Lewis: A Biography*. London: Collins, 1974.

- A.G. Herbert, *Liturgy and Society*. London: Faber and Faber, 1935.

- Richard W. Ladborough, "In Cambridge," James T. Como (ed.), *C.S. Lewis at the Breakfast Table and Other Reminiscnces*. New York: Macmillan, 1979.

- C.S. Lewis, *Mere Christianity*. New York: Macmillan, 1956.

- ————, *Letters to an American Lady*, Clyde S. Kilby (ed.). Grand Rapids, Michigan: Eerdmans, 1967.

- ————, *They Stand Together: The Letters of C.S. Lewis to Arthur Greeves (1914-63)*. Walter Hooper (ed.). New York: Macmillan, 1979.

- John Martin, "C.S. Lewis and Animals: The Road to Whipsnade," *C.S. Lewis: The Bulletin of the New York C.S. Lewis Society*, September 1993.

- George Musacchio, *C.S. Lewis, Man and Writer*. Belton, Texas: The University of Mary Hardin-Baylor, 1994.

- Robert Ross, "Afterword," *Household of God: A Parish History of St. Thomas's Church*. Toronto: St. Thomas's Church, 1993.

- George Sayer, "Jack on Holiday," James T. Como (ed.), C.S. *Lewis at the Breakfast Table and Other Reminiscences*. New York: Macmillan, 1979.

- —————, *Jack: C.S. Lewis and His Times*. San Francisco: Harper and Row, 1988.

- Dorothy L. Sayers, *The Nine Tailors*. London: Victor Gollancz, 1975.

- J.W.C. Wand, *Anglicanism in History and Today*. London: Weidenfeld and Nicholson, 1961.

- W. Gilbert Wilson, *The Faith of an Anglican*. Glasgow: Collins, 1980.

ASSESSING THE APOLOGETICS OF
C.S. LEWIS

By Clark H. Pinnock

For my money C.S. Lewis is the most effective Christian apologist of the twentieth century. He has done what he said he would do: "Ever since I became a Christian I have thought that the best, perhaps the only, service I could do for my unbelieving neighbours was to explain and defend the belief that has been common to nearly all Christians at all times."[1] Lewis has helped many to become Christians and many more to remain in the faith, and he continues to do this decades after his death. How is this possible? What are the strengths of his apologetic? What lessons can be drawn?

First, there is an appeal in his person. An apologist needs to be appealing as a human being as well as a thinker. Though in some ways a dull academic, in other ways his life was interesting to people outside the university. After all, he was a converted atheist, an Oxford scholar of English literature, a sound thinker, a good communicator orally and in print, a clear writer in various styles, a late-comer to romance, and a victim of a terrible grief. His life has been recorded in film and television specials and has been captured in numerous books for the coffee table. He is made more interesting by his associations with a remarkable circle of Christian communicators including Dorothy L. Sayers, J.R.R. Tolkien and Charles Williams, who were fascinating characters themselves.

Academically and personally, Lewis was well-endowed to become a good apologist because his defense of the gospel was much more than book learning—it arose out of life's struggles. It is obvious that he is not an ivory tower writer but a man with a passion who makes one want to know the God he knows.

A second strength lies in his theological ability. Lewis was a good writer who could make Christian doctrine interesting. It is surprising how keen people can be when doctrine is alive. Lewis did not give one the impression that his beliefs were a burden nor did he complain of the labours he expended in defending them. On the contrary, he found the doctrines to be compelling truths of contemporary relevance and he loved to commend them. Besides being enthusiastic, he was good at explaining why the miracles were important, how the Trinity is meaningful, what life after death might be like, what it means to pray, etc. He made Christian beliefs live as a good apologist should. If our message is not timely and gripping it is not worth the bother of defending. If, on the other hand, it has appeal, the effort to defend it becomes both pleasant and much simpler. Theologians as well as apologists can take a leaf out of Lewis's book and try to be interesting.

Sometimes an apologist needs to make decisions, because within tradition, doctrinal theories develop, not all of which deserve defending. For example, as an Anglican, Lewis did not have to defend papal infallibility or the immaculate conception of Mary, because they were not part of Christianity in his mind. He could sidestep the difficulties involved in defending them because they were superfluous. The point is that theological judgments precede apologetics and affect its agenda. The task is eased if the defects in theology are dispensed with first.

Lewis did not (I think) take many risks in the area. This is because he was a conservative and wanted to be as traditional as possible in all matters. Therefore, he tended to defend whatever came down to him as an Anglican layman from tradition. For example, regarding the nature of God, he retained the view that God is timeless and worked with it, even though it is dubiously scriptural and rationally mystifying. Regarding the doctrine of hell, he defended the traditional belief in the endless conscious torment of the wicked, even though the Bible often speaks of their destruction, and the moral problems with everlasting, conscious pain are immense. My point is that he did not normally question tradition but tired to make the best of it.

On a few subjects, though, he did introduce revisions and helped himself out apologetically. In eschatology, for example, he held to a wider hope and the possible salvation of the unevangelized. In *The Last Battle*[2] Emeth is saved by Aslan, even though during his lifetime he had worshipped Tash. This has not been the traditional view, though it is becoming a consensus. It illustrates that Lewis does not always choose the old over the new. Concerning the atonement, he does not seem to adhere to the penal substitutionary theory of the atonement as Calvin did, but seems closer to the theme of recapitulation found in Irenaeus and the Greek fathers. Remember how Lewis depicted Christ as the carrier of new life from whom we catch a good infection if we get close to him?[3] As for the nature of hell, he puts a kinder and gentler face upon it, even if it is still everlasting. He thought it possible that people might prefer hell to heaven and enjoy, among other things, the theological society which met on Thursdays in hell. This is not exactly what Augustine, Dante and Edwards thought the lake of fire would be like, though it makes better sense to most people nowadays. On the whole, Lewis underestimated the value of theological revision in the context of the apologetic task, though he sometimes engaged in it.

Another appeal of his apologetic is its cultural iconoclasm. It is incumbent on an apologist to know culture and be able to enter the experiential world of the audience. Lewis fulfils the requirement in his own way. He knows modern culture and *dislikes* it. Indeed he likened himself to a relic from a bygone age and a person trying to flag down the express train of modernity before it did more harm. He made it clear in his inaugural lecture at Cambridge and elsewhere that he did not advocate the cult of the new and that he thought the value of modernity greatly overestimated. Like other cultural critics, he thought that godlessness was leading society to the abolition of man and that God-centered thinking would be much more healthful. He reminds one of Orwell, Ellul, Solzhenitsyn, Muggeridge, Schaeffer, Bennett, etc., who sound the alarm concerning cultural drift and call us back to roots. His fear of collectivism, his distrust of authority, and his nonconformity all resonate with people.[4]

Lewis thus tapped into a vein of discontent with his negative view of social and cultural developments. He was an aware, conservative, counter-cultural, prophetic voice. Today he could be on talk radio or tread the conservative circuit. Being culturally sensitive as an apologist does not require approving of the leading trends. Raising a voice against trends can make one a hero. Old-fashioned views like hemlines have a way of becoming the leading fashion when things come round.

For me the greatest strength in C.S. Lewis as an apologist lies undoubtedly in his appeal *both* to reason and the imagination and to the recognition that Christianity is true *both* mythically and historically. This is a rare insight. Apologists so often sound like philosophers seeking logical arguments, as if they are what is most needed. They ignore the role of the imagination in faith and forget that the gospel is a mythic narrative. Lewis to his credit recognized that Christianity was both mythically and historically true and this is where his greatness lies.

Partly from training in English literature and partly from intuition, he sensed that God's truth comes alive for people through story as well as argument and he knew how to appeal to the affective side. He knew that a picture is worth a thousand words and that images, not arguments, sell products. The Narnia Chronicles are a most splendid work and they invite people to enter an imaginary world where they can experience Christian truth under the forms of fiction. It was brilliant of him to see that this is the way most people will begin to grasp what the Christian faith is about.

The Bible is full of stories and the power of its truth lies in narrative. Elie Wiesel once said that God created man because he loves stories. Lewis grasped that there is power in the myth as well as in the history of faith. Easter, for example, is a word of hope before it is ever proven to have happened, if it ever is so proven. Without diminishing the factual dimension, Lewis saw that the gospel is *myth made fact*, a blend of symbol and history. In contrast to traditionalists who ignore myth and liberals who ignore history, Lewis grasped the issue in its two-sidedness.[5]

There is psychological strength in this approach too. By appealing to the imagination, the apologist may secure a toehold in a person's consciousness before skepticism is given the opportunity to pounce.

And by then it can be too late because the fish is hooked. This approach may have come naturally to Lewis whose expertise lay in literature and the imagination already. Paradoxically, in appealing to the truth of story, Lewis is more post-modern than pre-modern, making him more than a mere traditionalist.

Controversy as well as appreciation surrounds his strictly rational apologetic. For all his love of the imagination, Lewis also insisted that faith was reasonable and could (and should) be defended against objections. Furthermore, he liked giving proofs for the existence of God and for all his beliefs. Like Pannenberg and unlike Barth, Lewis viewed theology as in search of universal truth and disliked fideism in religion heartily. A lot of us admire that about him.

Many readers appreciate the arguments they find in such books as *Mere Christianity, Miracles: A Preliminary Study*[6] and *The Problem of Pain.*[7] The arguments are attractively constructed and the ordinary reader (at least) is generally impressed by them. However, Lewis was not a professional philosopher like (say) Swinburne and there is controversy over how competent he was appealing to reason. Richard L. Purtill thinks the arguments are fundamentally sound though he improves them a little.[8] John Beversluis thinks Lewis claimed more than he could deliver by way of rationality and cuts him down to size.[9] A Lewis devotee will squirm uncomfortably reading Beversluis, but he makes one think.

Let us review the situation. First of all, Lewis did natural theology in his own particular way. He accepted the two-step approach: that one should first establish the existence of God before going on to argue on behalf of the claims of Christ. In his natural theology, though, he does not use the abstract forms of the traditional arguments but prefers more existentially gripping and modern (sic) forms of them. Thus we do not find the ontological, cosmological or teleological proofs in the way philosophers of religions generally discuss them but new versions of them. In this respect too Lewis was not just a traditionalist.

Most famously we come across the argument from desire in which Lewis plays upon dissatisfaction with the world and longing for God. It is an argument, not from objective features of the universe but from the experience of being human. For all his claim to be a relic of the past, Lewis participates in the modern turn to the subject in such a form of natural theology. It seems to me that the argument from desire is biblical in its appeal to the image of God in humans and perennially relevant, given the almost universal incidence of religion in culture. Granted, Lewis's own "desire" for God was temporarily confused by the awful experience described in *A Grief Observed*,[10] but it was not annihilated.

Lewis also makes use of the moral argument which is post-Kantian and not a traditional proof. He appealed to the fact that we render judgments about what is right and wrong, even about what is absolutely right or wrong, while at the same time experiencing moral failure and a need of divine grace. This is a powerful argument, whose weakness is the completeness of exposition at the hands of Lewis. The only alternative account of morality he discusses is ethical subjectivity, when in fact there are other theories to explain why there is morality. Though it could be said that Lewis did not aim at a complete account, I still get the feeling that he was too easily satisfied.

This is clearly true in the case of his argument from reason. How can thought result (he asked) from a purely material order? This is a good question except for the fact that Lewis went in the wrong direction. He questioned whether atheists had any right to trust the deliverances of their reason. In a famous debate on this matter, philosopher Elizabeth Anscombe noted flaws in his argument, how he went too far in claiming that atheists have no right to trust reason. He should have stuck with the issue of the origins of reason. A case can be made that mind makes more sense if God created the world than if the world evolved by chance. Rationality is certainly a surprising product of a purely material universe. This would be to use it as a form of the design argument. Even Purtill admits it was a misstep in argumentation. Lewis was careless in his reasoning, in overstating his case, and was chastened by the experience of a public refutation.

Regarding the incarnation, Lewis presented the famous trilemma: that the claims of Christ require one to decide whether Jesus was a lunatic, a liar or Lord. There is force to the argument in that during His lifetime, some thought Jesus to be a deceiver, while others considered Him mad, and still others worshipped Him. Jesus did tend to force people to decide concerning His identity. It is true that Lewis's arguments seldom lack a fundamental basis, even if too simply put. In this case, the situation is not quite as simple as he says. The "Jesus Seminar," for example, typical of liberal quest for the historical Jesus, would deny the authenticity of most of the sayings attributed to Jesus. This is a possibility which has to be addressed today but Lewis does not address it. It is not enough to say as he does: "I know myths when I see them and the gospels are not myths." The fact is that Lewis nowhere comes to grips with the challenge of New Testament research. He often seems to be satisfied with a simple form of his arguments. One feels a certain impatience when it comes to the details of his rational arguments. I am not saying that he himself had to go into biblical criticism. Someone else will certainly do it. What he must not do and what he does sometimes do is to give the impression that his argument is better than it is. That is not kosher.

What do I conclude in regard to rational apologetics of Lewis? I conclude two things. First, when he appeals to reason, his arguments are always suggestive but seldom complete. This became clear to Lewis himself in the debate with Anscombe in which he was simply shown to be wrong. Beversluis is right to say that the early Lewis appeared to think that he had a more effective logical apologetic than he did have. One could say that the audience he was targeting did not need more complicated arguments. That may be true, but I sense that he was impatient when it came to the details of rational apologetics. Although he had sound instincts in this area, he was content with elementary versions of arguments. The arguments, while valuable, suffer from a tendency to oversimplify.

Second, after the debate of 1948, Lewis did improve the argument from reason which Anscombe had demolished but also seems to place more energy in the apologetics of story, for which he was better prepared anyway. I believe Lewis is *more* effective when he appeals to the imagination than to reason. The debate of 1948 and the later experience of his wife's death made him aware of the limitations of rational argumentation when it comes to faith. His appeal to the imagination avoids these pitfalls and is in the end more effective.

The lesson I draw from this is that it is wiser to dwell upon the narrative proclamation rather than the nitty gritty questions of historical criticism or philosophical refinement. Lewis was dragged into seeing this and we should accept it. Not many apologists can do justice both to the grand mythical and the small factual detail. Ideally it would be nice to do them both well but it doesn't often happen. Someone like Wolfhart Pannenberg can do it but I have to ask myself, Is he as easy to read as Lewis? Certainly not.

The large Christian story possesses the power of truth apart from arguments and evidences. Arguments and evidences play a helping role when barriers to faith arise. But it is best to begin with the story and deal with the details later on.

CLARK H. PINNOCK

Clark H. Pinnock graduated from the University of Toronto with a B.A. in Semitic Languages in 1960 and the University of Manchester with a Ph.D. in New Testament in 1963. He taught at the University of Manchester (1963-65), New Orleans Baptist Theological Seminary (1965-69), Trinity Evangelical Divinity School (1969-1974), Regent College in Vancouver, British Columbia (1974-77), and since 1977 McMaster Divinity College in Hamilton, Ontario. Clark retired in 2002 and is now professor emeritus of theology.

He is author of a number of books including *Most Moved Mover: A Theology of God's Openness* (Baker Academic, 2001), *Flame of Love: A Theology of the Holy Spirit* (InterVarsity Press, 1996), and *A Wideness in God's Mercy: The Finality of Jesus Christ in a World of Religions* (Zondervan, 1992).

Clark is married to Dorothy and has a married daughter, Sarah Pinnock.

END NOTES

1. C.S. Lewis, *Mere Christianity* (New York: Macmillan Publishing Co., Inc., 1952), p. vi.

2. C.S. Lewis, *The Last Battle* (New York: Collier Books, 1956).

3. C.S. Lewis, *Mere Christianity*, p. 134-138.

4. See Richard B. Cunningham, *C.S. Lewis: Defender of the Faith* (Philadelphia: Westminster Press, 1967), ch. 2.

5. See Mark E. Freshwater, *C.S. Lewis and the Truth of Myth* (Lanham, MD: University Press of America, 1988.

6. C.S. Lewis, *Miracles: A Preliminary Study* (Great Britain: Fontana Books, 1960).

7. C.S. Lewis, *The Problem of Pain* (Great Britain: Fount Paperbacks, 1977).

8. Richard L. Purtill, C.S. Lewis's Case for the Christian Faith (San Francisco: Harper & Row, 1981).

9. John Beversluis, *C.S. Lewis and the Search for Rational Religion* (Grand Rapids: Eerdmans, 1985).

10. C.S. Lewis, *A Grief Observed* (San Francisco: HarperSanFrancisco, 1994).

C.S. LEWIS AS THE PATRON SAINT OF AMERICAN EVANGELICALISM*

By *Philip Graham Ryken*

Around the time Richard Attenborough's *Shadowlands* was released, A.N. Wilson was asked by the London *Times* about the phenomenal popularity of C.S. Lewis in America. Wilson—the Lewis biographer who has gone through a well-publicized anti-pilgrimage in the past decade—did not waste the opportunity to pour scorn on American evangelicals for their estimation of Lewis. "At Wheaton College in Illinois," he said, "where they are rather stupid fundamentalists, they have made C.S. Lewis into a god. They think he gives intellectual support for all their prejudices."

As is increasingly the case, Mr. Wilson's comments were not without their fair share of absurdity. Where most writers would have been content to let the word "fundamentalist" stand on its own, Wilson found it necessary to prefix the epithet "stupid." Furthermore, he gives more credit to Lewis's disciples than he is likely to have intended: "*They* think he gives intellectual support for all their prejudices." When put that way, it sounds as if those fundamentalists recognize their own prejudices and are committed to defending them on intellectual terms. But recognizing and defending prejudices are virtues rather than vices.

---

* This paper was first presented as a talk to the Oxford University C.S. Lewis Society, Hilary Term, 1995.

Yet Wilson's suggestion that American evangelicals have tried to make Lewis into a "god" comes close enough to the mark to pique one's interest. If evangelicals have not deified Lewis, have they at least canonized him? In other words, has C.S. Lewis become the patron saint of American evangelicalism?

This article attempts to explain the unusual place of C.S. Lewis in the American Church. It is a personal reflection rather than a scholarly analysis. I am an evangelical of evangelicals. I am also a product of Wheaton College (that home of "rather stupid fundamentalists"), raised virtually within the shadow of the Narnian wardrobe on Wheaton's campus. If C.S. Lewis is the patron saint of American evangelicalism, then he must be my patron saint as well.

A personal reflection is in keeping with my subject matter. American evangelicals tend towards an individualistic conception of Christianity. For me to offer my own perspective on C.S. Lewis, therefore, helps to prove my point. It shows how we have made him one of our own. To put this in the evangelical vernacular, this is a testimony of my personal relationship with C.S. Lewis.

At least five characteristics of Lewis's life and work account for his stature among American evangelicals. First, *the Britishness of C.S. Lewis*. Lewis evokes for Americans all the sophistication and quaintness of England. To read Lewis is to enter a world where school children wait on railway platforms at the end of their holidays or crawl from attic to attic in London rowhouses. It is a world where people use torches instead of flashlights and listen to the wireless rather than the radio. It is a world where, wonder of wonders, Turkish Delight is available in all the shops!

What is of even more consequence is the fact that Lewis was an Oxford don. For Americans, Oxford is the quintessence of England.

> [O]ur national romance with Oxford has less to do with
> its alumni than with our Bridesheadish image of the place: its
> aura of tweedy erudition, its dewy green fields, gargoyles
> frowning from the turrets of medieval buildings, and all those
> pipe-smoking lads in white pants and thick sweaters debating

the merits of Gibbon and Eliot (David Segal, "Oxford: An Excellent Adventure," *The American Oxonian*, 80:1, p. 15).

If this image of Oxford had begun to fade from American consciousness, then the movie *Shadowlands*, with its scenes of quiet Magdalen cloisters, sophisticated Randolph teas, jocular High Table debates, and raucous undergraduates hurling themselves into the Isis has perpetuated the Oxford mystique for another generation.

The Britishness of C.S. Lewis is a necessary but insufficient condition for his popularity in America. His reputation also has something to do with *the love of allegory*. American evangelicalism has an uneasy conscience about the arts. The artistic genre within which evangelicals feel most readily at home is allegory. For instance, the one literary production which received instant acclaim and exercised enduring theological influence within evangelical circles in England and America was John Bunyan's *Pilgrim's Progress*. Apart from artistic or literary considerations, allegories can always be justified on doctrinal or pedagogical grounds.

Lewis himself had reservations about allegory, if by allegory one means a work of art in which central characters and episodes display direct correspondence with theological truths. With the exception of *The Pilgrim's Regress: An Allegorical Apology for Christianity, Reason and Romanticism*, his novels are not allegories. The fiction of C.S. Lewis has more depth than that. The relationship between his art and his theology is more complex, more probing. His narratives are mythical rather than allegorical. They evoke rather than articulate Christian doctrine.

Even if Lewis himself would bristle at the suggestion that his fictional works are allegorical, the works themselves are saturated with doctrinal themes. *Out of the Silent Planet* explores the doctrine of the incarnation; *Perelandra (Voyage to Venus)* portrays the fall from innocence into experience; *The Lion, the Witch and the Wardrobe* offers a fair summary of the doctrine of substitutionary atonement; *The Last Battle* is a digest of Christian eschatology; and so on. It is not just that Lewis's fiction coheres with a theistic worldview. The central tenets of Christian doctrine echo and reverberate in his stories.

To the biblically-literate Christian, theological themes are easy to detect in Lewis's fiction. Even A.N. Wilson's stupid fundamentalist is likely to have a doxastic moment when he reads *The Magician's Nephew* and sees Jadis clambering over the garden wall and wiping forbidden juice from her dark lips. As Lewis admitted, this is a picture of "what happens to those who pluck and eat fruits at the wrong time and in the wrong way."

Lewis once attempted to coax an American schoolgirl into another moment of theological recognition:

> As to Aslan's other name, well, I want you to guess. Has there never been anyone in *this* world who (1) arrived at the same time as Father Christmas (2) Said he was the Son of the Great Emperor (3) Gave himself up for someone else's fault to be jeered at and killed by wicked people (4) Came to life again (5) Is sometimes spoken of as a Lamb (at the end of the *Dawn Treader*)? Don't you really know His name in this world? Think it over and let me know your answer! (Lyle W. Dorsett and Marjorie Lamp Mead, eds., *C.S. Lewis: Letters to Children*, New York: Simon and Schuster, 1985, p. 32).

That Lewis was willing to spell things out like this shows that the Narnia Chronicles are large-print editions of Christian myth. And to Lewis's claim that "any amount of theology can be smuggled into people's minds under cover of romance without their knowing it," the evangelical utters a heartfelt, "Amen."

It must he admitted that there are several respects in which Lewis's brand of Christianity seems incompatible with mainstream American evangelicalism. Despite his defense of the historicity of the gospels, Lewis is weak on the inerrancy of Scripture, reaching the baffling conclusion in his *Reflections on the Psalms* that error, contradiction, and even wickedness have not been removed from the Bible. At the same time, to many evangelicals he seems overly strong on so-called Christian liberties. Lewis once suggested that "many who find that 'nothing happens' when they sit down, or kneel down, to a book of devotion, would find that the heart sings unbidden while they are working their way through a tough bit of theology with a pipe in their teeth and a pencil in their hand." If evangelicals have followed this advice, most have done so without the pipe.

Lewis's perceived weaknesses have not tarnished his reputation. Walter Hooper recounts the story of the visit paid to Lewis by the well-known American fundamentalist, Bob Jones. Upon his return, Jones said, "Well, he drinks, he smokes, but I think that man's a Christian!"

Evangelicals like Bob Jones have been willing to overlook Lewis's flaws—even to learn from some of them—because he is strong on a cluster of theological distinctives that lie at the heart of evangelical theology. Many doctrines might be included in this context, but I mention one of the most important: conversion, or the new birth. American evangelicals are **not surprised by** *Surprised by Joy*.

Being born again may not be a particularly strong theme in Lewis's writings as a whole. Certainly a large share of his apologetic work—the radio talks that eventuated in *Mere Christianity*, for example—had as its ultimate purpose the conversion of sinners from unbelief to belief in Christ. As Lewis wrote in *God in the Dock: Essays on Theology and Ethics*, "Most of my books are evangelistic." But much of his apologetic work has an off-hand style about it, as if to say: "Look here, Christianity seems ever so reasonable to me, and here's why, but you can take it or leave it." His apologetic method sometimes lacks the "You must be born again" asseveration of Jesus in the Gospels.

Yet Lewis's own *experience* of conversion from atheism to orthodoxy is sufficient to establish his evangelical *bona fides*. The story of his discovery that "all my writings and watchings for Joy ... had been a futile attempt to contemplate the enjoyed" is well-known to American evangelicals:

> The odd thing was that before God closed in on me, I was in fact offered what now appears a moment of wholly free choice. In a sense. I was going up Headington Hill on the top of a bus. Without words and (I think) almost without images, a fact about myself was somehow presented to me. I became aware that I was holding something at bay, or shutting something out (*Surprised by Joy*, London: Geoffrey Bles, 1955, p. 211).

Lewis continues:

> You must picture me alone in that room in Magdalen, night after night, feeling, whenever my mind lifted for even a second from my work, the steady, unrelenting approach of Him whom I so earnestly desired not to meet. That which I greatly feared had at last come upon me. In the Trinity Term of 1929 I gave in, and admitted that God was God, and knelt and prayed; perhaps, that night, the most dejected and reluctant convert in all England (p. 215).

In earlier generations, John Wesley's testimony of his heart "strangely warmed" was the paradigmatic account of Christian conversion. Lewis's surprising encounter with joy has risen to similar prominence in the evangelical understanding of what it means to be born again. Listen long enough and someone will say, perhaps unwittingly: "and there I was, the most reluctant convert in all Cleveland ... or Topeka ... or Kalamazoo."

Closely related to Lewis's account of conversion is his powerful presentation of the life of close fellowship with God. He knows what it means to have what evangelicals term a "personal relationship with Jesus Christ."

Of all the characters in Lewis's novels, Lucy best exemplifies the reverence and joy at heart of the Christian faith. Lucy was the first to go into Narnia, the first to meet Aslan, the first to recognize him when the Pevensies returned, and the first to detect his silver outline in the moonlight. How did she know it was Aslan? "He—I—I just know," said Lucy, "by his face." It was Lucy who first wept over Aslan's carcase, ran her fingers through his mane, and romped with him. It was Lucy's prayer to Aslan, whispered in the darkness, that summoned an albatross to lead the *Dawn Treader* to safety. Even Lucy's awful chastisement from Aslan, after looking in the magician's forbidden book on the island of the monopods, had the same mixture of reverence and compassion. To the fullest measure, Lucy had exactly the kind of relationship with Aslan which evangelicals envisage when they speak of having a personal relationship with Jesus Christ.

For the dutiful evangelical, there is no substitute for nurturing one's relationship with Christ by maintaining a daily quiet time of prayer and Bible reading. Not surprisingly, C.S. Lewis seems to have recognized the necessity of daily devotions. In *The Silver Chair*, Jill is given four signs to guide her on her quest to rescue Prince Rilian from captivity. She is to recite them morning and evening, lest she forget them. What Lewis is *really* talking about, the evangelical suspects, is daily devotions. Can you remember the four signs Jill was given? If not, you can see the fate which befalls those who neglect their Quiet Times!

The decision to take these examples from Lewis's so-called children's fiction rather than his theological writings is deliberate. More than anything else, it is Lewis's children's literature which has secured his prominence in America. While there are signs that many of his apologetic arguments are losing their forcefulness in a pluralistic culture, it seems unlikely that the Narnia Chronicles will fall out of favour, at least while the West remains literate. C.S. Lewis is the patron saint of American evangelicalism because he is *fun for the whole family*.

I first encountered *The Lion, the Witch and the Wardrobe* before I was able to read it for myself. Even before that time, I heard the name of C.S. Lewis uttered in reverential tones. If he was not a family member, he was at least someone we knew well.

My own love for the Narnia Chronicles as stories was instant. I can remember the resentment with which I greeted my mother's attempts to see, from time to time, if I was catching the spiritual meanings—not to say allegorical meanings—which lay beneath the surface of the narratives. But I was not about to allow the stories to be ruined by figuring out what they meant.

Once I was able to read the stories for myself, I associated them with being in bed. I did not have a really satisfactory illness unless I had time to read all seven Narnia Chronicles, either in canonical or chronological order. (One result is that the illness of Digory's mother in *The Magician's Nephew* has always elicited a response of deep empathy.)

Since my father is a member of the English Department at Wheaton College I was also afforded the privilege of examining the Lewis artifacts which belong to Wheaton's Marion E. Wade Centre. These relics include the original manuscript and drawings of the *Boxen* stories Lewis wrote when he was a child.

More impressive than Lewis's juvenilia was the richly carved and ornamented wardrobe which then guarded the entrance to the English Department. It was, of course, *the* wardrobe which had belonged to Lewis's grandfather and had been shipped from Belfast for reassembly. Westmont College in California rescued a second wardrobe from the Kilns, Lewis's home near Oxford. At Wheaton we have always recognized the Westmont wardrobe as an impostor, although some insist that the Westmont wardrobe more closely matches the description in *The Lion, the Witch and the Wardrobe*. In any case, that Lewis's personal effects can arouse such an argument demonstrates that he has become the patron saint of American evangelicalism. Few things convey legitimacy upon a potential saint as effectively as disputed relics.

Although the wardrobe at Wheaton was kept closed (for safety?), I could hardly walk by it without experiencing a *frisson* of anxiety. Did my father ever step into it for Narnian adventures? After all, who would ever know, since Narnian time does not consume any earth time? Or perhaps recalcitrant college students were muscled into the wardrobe for a dose of the Eustace treatment. Given such imaginative stimuli, it was little wonder that C.S. Lewis seemed like a family member.

Even at an early age, I was aware that C.S. Lewis was equally fun for the rest of the family. The ritual of Christmas morning included three obligatory presents for my grandfather: a bag of lemon drops, an inedible fruitcake, and a new hardback volume of C.S. Lewis. "That's great!" he would say, a grin spreading across his face. It was the defining moment of Christmas morning.

C.S. Lewis was fun for my grandmother as well. Although she taught elementary school mathematics, *The Lion, the Witch and the Wardrobe* afforded her the opportunity to conduct a campaign of covert evangelism in the public school classroom. Unschooled in the ways of myth, liberal

American educators could scarcely have appreciated the danger of allowing Lewis into the classroom. Fun for the whole family indeed!

Lewis has been most fun of all for my father, himself a literary critic, Milton scholar, and interpreter of culture in Christian perspective. The thought of C.S. Lewis features prominently in his lectures and books on *Paradise Lost*, Renaissance literature, and the literature of the Bible. And the fun seems likely to continue, especially now that my firstborn is happily through his first hearing of the Narnia Chronicles.

The point of mentioning all the fun we have had with C.S. Lewis is simply to show the breadth of his appeal. There are many Lewises to love. If an evangelical does not have an appetite for fantasy or science fiction, he or she will at least have an appetite for Lewis's apologetics or literary criticism.

The breadth of Lewis's appeal may account for his dominance in evangelical circles. One can scarcely read a magazine or listen to a sermon without hearing a quotation from C.S. Lewis. What evangelical has not heard Lewis's account of his conversion, or his "further up, further in" description of heaven in *The Last Battle*, or the "liar, lunatic or Lord" trilemma from *Mere Christianity*, or any number of other well-known quotations from his writings? Already in the 1970s, Michael J. Christensen observed that "it is quite fashionable these days to quote Lewis on any number of theological subjects as an authority approaching that of a church father." The Lewis quotation is the religious equivalent of the political sound byte, and every bit as American.

Several examples may help illustrate the ubiquity of *The Quotable Lewis*. Exhibit A comes from that eminent journal of American letters, *Sports Illustrated*. A 1981 article on the Tasmanian devil opens and closes with references to "the English natural philosopher and novelist C.S. Lewis." Less surprising, but more telling, is the prominent place given to Lewis in Richard Foster's 1990 anthology of *Devotional Classics*. The first entry in the book does not come from Augustine or Gregory of Nyssa, but from C.S. Lewis. In the *milieu* of American evangelicalism, this seems fitting; it serves as an imprimatur for the whole volume.

Or consider this example, culled from the introduction to an article on the American Academy of Religion: "In the halls of academe," writes the editor of the evangelical news magazine *World*, "religion is just one more sociological phenomenon, to be appraised from a safe distance." A parenthesis follows: "After all, He may not be a *tame* lion." That this is an allusion to Aslan is self-evident; there is no need to unpack the allusion. The editor can assume that the evangelical reader will have read Lewis and recognized that Aslan is a cipher for God.

A recent issue of a more substantive publication, *Modern Reformation*, contains several references to Lewis. First, in an article on theological method, portions of Lewis's *Miracles: A Preliminary Study* and his *Selected Literary Essays* are quoted. Later in the same issue appears the full text of Lewis's introduction to *St. Athanasius on the Incarnation*. That Athanasius himself may be unfamiliar to some readers is evident from the fact that he is mistakenly identified as "St. Anthansius." No matter: the piece itself is written by C.S. Lewis. Him we know.

A final example comes from *Citizen*, a magazine published by the evangelical ministry, *Focus on the Family*. *Citizen* advocates traditional family values from a Christian perspective. And who better to advise American Christians about how to conduct themselves in the public arena than C.S. Lewis? Thus *Citizen* prints an article entitled "Recruiting C.S. Lewis for today's culture war." The subtitle assures readers that this "Christian author offered ideas that may be helpful to pro-family activists."

The picture is worth a thousand words. C.S. Lewis sits at his desk with a handkerchief tucked tidily in his jacket pocket and a pipe resting on the corner of his desk. In his hand he holds, not a fountain pen, but a computer mouse. A large computer terminal dominates the desk. This is a C.S. Lewis for our times, a man seemingly at home on the information superhighway at the start of the millennium.

The blurb at the beginning of the article notes that "Lewis is best known...for providing the intellectual underpinnings of Christian faith." Not with identifying or explaining the underpinnings of the Christian faith, notice, but actually for *providing* them. Chalk one up for A.N. Wilson, who was the first to notice the relationship between

Lewis and intellectual underpinnings. We have moved beyond canonization to deification.

What follows is an interview in which *Citizen* poses the questions and Lewis provides the answers. "What role do you believe religious faith should play in contemporary American politics?" "Now that President Clinton and other liberal elitists have begun talking about 'family values,' how can pro-family activists avoid being duped?" And so forth. With brilliant foresight, Lewis anticipates these uniquely American difficulties and provides answers from his published works.

Depending on one's point of view, the use of C.S. Lewis to address the particulars of American politics is either the apotheosis or the nadir of the quotable Lewis. Even if one is sympathetic to the evangelical embrace of Lewis, it is good to be reminded of the chief danger of hagiography: worshiping the saint rather than the Sanctifier.

There is also the danger of refashioning the saint into one's own image. It is this danger which particularly afflicts enthusiasts of C.S. Lewis, whether they view him as more or less an evangelical, a middle-of-the-road Anglican, a Roman Catholic, or even a theologically-ambivalent Protestant. To the extent that Christians see their own reflection when they gaze at Lewis, they are not worshiping God, or even Lewis, but themselves.

The irony of the tendency to read Lewis on one's own terms is that this is the antithesis of the kind of reading he championed. In his *Experiment in Criticism*, Lewis writes of the difference between the many and the few, between unliterary and literary readers, between those who use art and those who receive it.

To explain the difference, Lewis considers several possible readings of Tintoretto's *Three Graces*. It would be possible, of course, to view the work as a representation of classical mythology, or as pornography. But to view it in either of these ways is to *misuse* it. Lewis offers an alternative:

> Real appreciation demands the opposite process. We must not let loose our own subjectivity upon the pictures and make them its vehicles. We must begin by laying aside as completely as we can all our own preconceptions, interests, and

associations. We must make room for Botticelli's Mars and Venus...by emptying our own. After the negative effort, the positive. We must use our eyes. We must look, and go on looking till we have certainly seen exactly what is there. We sit down before the picture in order to have something done to us, not that we may do things with it. The first demand any work of any art makes upon us is surrender. Look. Listen. Receive. Get yourself out of the way. (There is no good asking first whether the work before you deserves such a surrender, for until you have surrendered you cannot possibly find out) (Cambridge University Press, 1961, pp. 18-19).

It is this kind of reading which C.S. Lewis not only demands, but also deserves. He can only be embraced—or rejected—when he has been heard as he is, not as one might like him to be. We should not read Lewis to do things with him, but for him to do something to us.

PHILIP GRAHAM RYKEN

Philip Graham Ryken is Senior Minister of Tenth Presbyterian Church in Philadelphia, Pennsylvania, where he has preached since 1995. He is Bible Teacher for the Alliance of Confessing Evangelicals, speaking nationally on the radio program *Every Last Word*. Dr. Ryken was educated at Wheaton College, Wheaton, Illinois; Westminster Theological Seminary, Glenside, Pennsylvania; and the University of Oxford (United Kingdom), from which he received his doctorate in historical theology. He lives with his wife (Lisa) and children (Joshua, Kirsten, Jack, Kathryn and Karoline) in Center City, Pennsylvania. When he is not preaching or playing with his family, he likes to read books, shoot baskets, and ponder the relationship between Christian faith and American culture. He has written or edited more than twenty books, including *The Message of Salvation*, *The Doctrines of Grace* (with James Montgomery Boice), and *City on a Hill: Reclaiming the Biblical Pattern for the Church in the Twenty-first Century*.

DEATH AND DYING IN THE WRITINGS OF C.S. LEWIS

By Peter J. Schakel

D epicting death is a tricky matter for a fiction writer. A dramatist can enact death on the stage. But writers of fiction encounter more difficulty, particularly in conveying the death of the central character, the one from whose perspective the action is related and whose viewpoint we have come to share. The death of other characters (those we see from the outside) can be described—but what about the death of a point-of-view character? Margaret Doody, writing on 18th- and 19th-century novels, explains the problem this way: death is the ultimate reality. Characters in fiction are imaginary. Deaths in fiction are difficult because they create moments of transparency: they reveal that the fiction is a fiction. We know that the deaths are not real—the characters never lived, so they cannot die; if they do die, we can bring them back to life by rereading the work.[1] Like every serious author, C.S. Lewis faced the problem of writing about death. This paper will examine how he dealt with the problem: first, how he described death in nonfictional writings, then how he depicted it in fiction. My thesis is that Lewis consistently treats death as a factual reality (death is a fact of life, we all will die sometime, Christians especially should not fear death), not an emotional reality (not writing publicly about the emotional effect of death until A Grief Observed).

From early in his life, C.S. Lewis encountered death a number of times. The deaths of his mother in 1908 (when Lewis was ten), his father in 1929, his close friend Charles Williams in 1945, and his wife Joy Davidman in 1960, all affected him deeply and are pivotal events punctuating his life at roughly equal intervals. It is not surprising that references to and discussions of death run through Lewis's autobiography, *Surprised by Joy: The Shape of My Early Life*, as a unifying motif, and they offer a valuable point from which to consider the way he wrote about death.

At the end of the opening chapter of *Surprised by Joy* Lewis tells of his mother's death: "There came a night when I was ill and crying both with headache and toothache and distressed because my mother did not come to me. That was because she was ill too; and what was odd was that there were several doctors in her room, and voices and comings and goings all over the house and doors shutting and opening. It seemed to last for hours. And then my father, in tears, came into my room and began to try to convey to my terrified mind things it had never conceived before. It was in fact cancer and followed the usual course; an operation..., an apparent convalescence, a return of the disease, increasing pain, and death. My father never fully recovered from this loss."[2] The last sentence seems striking to me: not *I* never fully recovered from this loss, though there is every reason to believe it deeply affected the rest of his life. Instead he shifts attention to his father. He goes on in the next paragraph to talk at length about his father's grieving and its effect on Lewis and his brother, which makes it seem as if he has talked about the effect of her death on himself, though he hasn't really.

The account of his mother's death begins two paragraphs after, and thus is juxtaposed with, Lewis's lengthy description of his third glimpse of joy, which resulted from reading these lines from Longfellow's translation of *Tegner's Drapa*: "Balder the beautiful/Is dead, is dead." The structure of the text thus makes it seem as if the fictional death moved him more than the actual one—I suspect in fact it is just that he found the fictional death easier to talk about than the actual one. But the effort to avoid discussing a long-term emotional effect on himself is clear. He goes so far as admitting grief: "For us boys the real bereavement had happened before our mother died. We lost her gradually as she was gradually withdrawn from our life into the hands of nurses and delirium and morphia..." (*SJ* 18-19); but even that becomes a way to deny a continuing effect. The paragraph in which he says the most also suggests, through its reserved tone and powerful metaphors, how much goes unsaid: "With my mother's death all settled happiness, all that was tranquil and reliable, disappeared from my life.... [N]o more of the old security. It was sea and islands now; the great continent had sunk like Atlantis" (*SJ* 21).

Near the end of the book he relates his father's death in one sentence: "My father's death, with all the fortitude (even playfulness) which he displayed in his last illness, does not really come into the story I am telling" (*SJ* 215). Two things stand out here. One is the attention he gives to his father's fortitude and playfulness: this is the way death is to be approached, as a factual reality, to be faced without fear or rebellion. The other is his claim that his father's death "does not really come into the story I am telling," the story of his reconversion. George Sayer's biography calls this claim into question: "Albert's death affected Jack profoundly. He could no longer be in rebellion against the political churchgoing that was part of his father's way of life. He felt bitterly ashamed of the way he had deceived and denigrated his father in the past.... Most importantly, he had a strong feeling that Albert was somehow still alive and helping him."[3] It is notable—and consistent with his way of writing about death—that Lewis's own account determinedly avoids admitting the emotional reality.

In a key passage of *Surprised by Joy* Lewis claims that he always viewed death only as a factual reality. The passage occurs in his description of his experience as a soldier in World War I.[4] After he was hit by a bullet and found (or thought he found) that he was not breathing, he "concluded that this was death. I felt no fear and certainly no courage. It did not seem to be an occasion for either. The proposition 'Here is a man dying' stood before my mind as dry, as factual, as unemotional as something in a textbook. It was not even interesting" (*SJ* 197). This seems to me an entirely believable reaction to the shock of being hit by a bullet. But I question whether it really was the only and lasting reaction. The *Surprised by Joy* account indicates that it was: with cool detachment Lewis uses the experience of being wounded as grist for his later understanding of the distinction between Kant's Noumenal and Phenomenal selves. It is the ultimate example of his treatment of death always as a factual reality, not admitting it to have emotional reality.[5] At the beginning of *Surprised by Joy* Lewis contrasts the two different strains in his ancestry, the Lewises, whom he describes as highly emotional, "sentimental, passionate, and rhetorical" (*SJ* 3) and the Hamiltons, whom he describes as "a cooler race," tranquil, critical, ironic (*SJ* 3). David C. Downing, in his fine book *Planets in Peril: A Critical Study of C.S. Lewis's Ransom Trilogy*, points out that this analysis is not historically accurate, that the important thing is what it reveals about Lewis—his deep desire to be what the Hamiltons stood for to him.[6] The persona he develops in *Surprised by Joy* embodies those Hamiltonian traits, of being cool, collected, in control; and nothing in the book reflects them better than the description he gives of his reaction to the thought that he was dying.

The detached attitude in *Surprised by Joy* is consistent with Lewis's practical, no nonsense approach to death in his essays and letters: face the facts, we're all going to die sometime, get on with life and don't fret about death. Christians, especially, should not fear death, but accept it, if not welcome it. Typical is his answer to the question "How are we to live in an atomic age": "do not let us begin by exaggerating the novelty of our situation. Believe me, dear sir or madam, you and all whom you love were already sentenced to death before the atomic age was invented: and quite a high percentage of us were going to die in unpleasant ways."[7] Likewise, this passage from an interview in May 1963: "I find it difficult to keep from laughing when I find people worrying about future destruction of some kind or other. [Don't] they know they [are] going to die anyway? Apparently not. My wife once asked a young woman friend whether she had ever thought of death, and she replied, 'By the time I reach that age science will have done something about it!'"[8]

In light of his handling of death in these essays and *Surprised by Joy*, it is interesting and instructive to pay attention to deaths in Lewis's fiction. Deaths occur often, almost always as factual, not emotional, realities. Often the deaths occur to minor characters, those we see from the outside, whose deaths can be described objectively. And usually those deaths occur by agency: Wormwood's patient dies in *The Screwtape*

Letters; Hyoi, the *hross*, is shot from a distance by the villains in *Out of the Silent Planet*; the evil Unman is strangled by Ransom in *Perelandra: Voyage to Venus*; Hingest, the good scientist, is bludgeoned to death by assassins in *That Hideous Strength: A Modern Fairy-Tale for Grown-Ups*; talking animals and some human characters die in battle in the Chronicles of Narnia. Repeatedly Lewis's works demonstrate, or urge, acceptance of death. An important theme in *Out of the Silent Planet*, for example, is Ransom's need to overcome fear of death. The Oyarsa tells Ransom, in a key paragraph, "one thing we left behind us on the *harandra*: fear.... The weakest of my people does not fear death."[9]

In some cases, the fictional works back away from depicting a death experience—Ransom, the central character in *Out of the Silent Planet*, *Perelandra* and *That Hideous Strength*, is translated to another world without dying.

> "He will be with Arthur, certainly, [in the Third Heaven, in Perelandra]," said Dimble.... "There are people who have never died. We do not yet know why. We know a little more than we did about the How. There are many places in the universe—I mean, this same physical universe in which our planet moves—where an organism can last practically forever."[10]

In so doing, Lewis links Ransom to biblical characters—Enoch, Elijah—who do not go through death, and to Arthur, central figure in the romances Lewis loved.[11] But he also avoids the necessity of handling the death of a character with whom readers relate closely, one whose death could break the spell of this "Modern Fairy-Tale for Grown-Ups" and plunge readers into real emotions over a fictional character.

Lewis also backs away from depicting death in *The Magician's Nephew*. Digory Kirke's mother is seriously ill and near death. In our first glimpse of him his face is as grubby as if he had rubbed his hands in the earth, and then had a good cry, and then dried his face with his hands, which, as a matter of fact, is very nearly what he had been doing. He then pours out many frustrations to Polly, but particularly that his "Mother [is] ill and [is] going to—going to—die."[12] Here, in a fictional character, we get a glimpse of the emotions the young Lewis himself felt, but which the older Lewis could not allow himself to describe in *Surprised by Joy*. Here, in his fiction, we come close to touching death as an emotional reality.

Lewis may have been able to come that close because the story was not going to end with death. Later in the story Digory overhears his aunt say, "Poor, dear little Mabel! I'm afraid it would need fruit from the land of youth to help her now. Nothing in *this* world will do much." Digory, transported to Narnia by means of magic rings fashioned by his mad-magician uncle, meets the great lion Aslan and asks Aslan to give him something that will cure his mother.

> [H]e looked up at [the Lion's] face. What he saw surprised him as much as anything in his whole life. For the tawny face was bent down near his own and (wonder of wonders) great shining tears stood in the Lion's eyes. They were such big, bright tears compared with Digory's own that for a moment he felt as if the Lion must really be sorrier about his Mother than he was himself.
>
> "My son, my son," said Aslan. "I know. Grief is great. Only you and I in this land [the newly created Narnia] know that yet. Let us be good to one another" (*MN* 142).

Rather than give him a cure, Aslan sends him on a quest, to find and bring back an apple that will protect and preserve Narnia from evil for many years. When Digory finds the magic apple, a wicked witch urges him not to bring it to Aslan but to take it home because it has the power to make his mother well again. Digory is faced with a "most terrible choice" (*MN* 162), but he resists the temptation and returns to Aslan. From the apple grows a tree which protects Narnia from the wicked witch for centuries. And from the tree Aslan gives Digory an apple to take back to his mother. She eats the apple and, "no sooner had she finished it than she smiled and her head sank back on the pillow and she was asleep: a real, natural, gentle sleep, without any of those nasty drugs" (*MN* 181). The next day the doctor examines her and tells Aunt Letty, "this is the most extraordinary case I have known in my whole medical career. It is—it is like a miracle" (*MN* 182). Within a month Digory's mother is well again. His father inherits a fortune, and they move to a great big house in the country, and they all live happily ever after.

Compare these events with Lewis's account of his own situation when he was Digory's age: "When her case was pronounced hopeless I remembered what I had been taught; that prayers offered in faith would be granted. I accordingly set myself to produce by will power a firm belief that my prayers for her recovery would be successful; and, as I thought, I achieved it. When nevertheless she died I shifted my ground and worked myself into a belief that there was to be a miracle" (SJ 20). The young Lewis prayed to God as to a magician, and his prayer was not successful. Typical of *Surprised by Joy*, no emotion is mentioned, and a lesson is drawn consistent with the book's death-as-factual-reality motif: "The interesting thing is that my disappointment produced no results beyond itself. The thing hadn't worked, but I was used to things not working, and I thought no more about it.... I had approached God, or my idea of God, without love, without awe, even without fear. He was, in my mental picture of this miracle, to appear neither as Saviour nor as Judge, but merely as a magician; and when He had done what was required of Him I supposed He would simply—well, go away. It never crossed my mind that the tremendous contact which I solicited should have any consequences beyond restoring the *status quo*. I imagine that a 'faith' of this kind is often generated in children and that its disappointment is of no religious importance" (SJ 20-21). Two things strike me here. One is the extent to which this passage reflects the older Lewis looking back and filling in theological understandings that wouldn't have occurred to the young Lewis. The second is Lewis's assertion that the episode was of no future religious importance: for him not to concede an effect on his subsequent loss of faith seems to me a further example of his resistance to death as emotional reality and of his need throughout *Surprised by Joy* to shape his story to fit the way he had come to remember or interpret it.

In *The Magician's Nephew* Lewis set up a situation in which the natural, realistic outcome would be the death of the mother of the character from whose viewpoint we have read the story, as it happened with his own mother. He even set up the sympathetic, empathetic, Aslan as a way of illustrating to children a positive response to grief.

Then, he backed away from that ending, for various possible reasons. One is generic. As in *That Hideous Strength*, a death at the end would have brought the fairy tale crashing down to reality. Another is his own reserve: to include the mother's death would force him to depict the son's grief, and even in fiction that would be too revealing of his emotions surrounding the death of his own mother. Whatever the reason, the result is that he transforms, and enriches, his own experience into a retelling of the Garden of Eden story, with profound moral and spiritual meaning. The encounter with the witch over the apple turns into a confrontation over promises made and kept or not kept, with a great deal riding on Digory's keeping of his promise: the future of Narnia hangs in the balance, as well as the fate of Digory and his mother. If he had stolen the apple, it would have healed Digory's mother, "but not to your joy or hers. The day would have come when both you and she would have looked back and said it would have been better to die in that illness" (*MN* 175). Once again, death is presented as a reality that must be accepted. But, in this case, because the promise was kept, death is avoided: the story turns from tragedy (from death, and the emotions Lewis avoids depicting) to *eucatastrophe*, that is, in J.R.R. Tolkien's words, "sudden and miraculous grace: never to be counted on to recur," "the joy of deliverance" with its promise of the final victory of the good.[13]

It would, admittedly, have been difficult to include in a children's story the death of the mother of the perspective character. But as imaginative a writer as surely Lewis could have found a way to do so. He did, after all, find a creative way to convey death in the next book, *The Last Battle*. *The Last Battle* achieves an extraordinary feat: in a children's story, it depicts the death in battle of the characters readers have been closest to throughout the book, Tirian, Jill and Eustace. Lewis obviously cannot have perspective characters experience an arrow piercing their skin or a sword being run through them, the way he can describe it for the animals around them. Instead, he achieves his result in two ways. First, through symbolism: Tirian, Jill and Eustace are thrown through a door into a stable. The door is referred to as a "dark door," a "grim door...more like a mouth."[14] One character passed through it and appeared to be thrown back out, dead. Other characters went through the door and did not return. Poggin the Dwarf thinks that "we shall all, one by one, pass through that dark door before morning. I can think of a hundred deaths I would rather have died" (*LB* 128). But the door turns from a terrifying image to another instance of *eucatastrophe*, giving a glimpse of the Joy beyond the walls of the world (Tolkien 81): thus Jewel adds, "It may be for us the door to Aslan's country and we shall sup at his table tonight" (*LB* 128). When Jill, Tirian and Eustace are thrown through the door, they find themselves in the New Narnia, in heaven. Lewis skillfully engages his viewpoint characters in a "last battle," a battle to the death for those on the losing side, but finds a way to present their deaths to young readers as a potentially fearful and tragic, but ultimately positive and joyful, experience.

A second way he conveys the death of viewpoint characters is by having the deaths of Jill and Eustace occur in our world in a train wreck. The characters raise the question of what will happen in our world if they are killed in the Narnian world: "Shall we wake up and find ourselves back in that train [from which they were pulled into Narnia]? Or shall we just vanish and never be heard of any more? Or shall we be dead in England?" (*LB* 96). They reflect that it will be nasty for their loved ones in our world if they just disappear, without a trace. Then Jill continues:

> "I *was* going to say I wished we'd never come. But I don't, I don't, I don't. Even if we *are* killed. I'd rather be killed fighting for Narnia than grow old and stupid at home and perhaps go about in a bathchair and then die in the end just the same."
>
> "Or be smashed up by British Railways!"
>
> "Why d'you say that?"
>
> "Well when that awful jerk came—the one that seemed to throw us into Narnia—I thought it *was* the beginning of a railway accident. So I was jolly glad to find ourselves here instead" (*LB* 96-97).

At the end of the book, as they bask in the wonder of the New Narnia, Aslan tells them that there was a wreck and they did die in it:

> "There *was* a real railway accident," said Aslan softly. "Your father and mother and all of you are—as you used to call it in

the Shadow-Lands—dead. The term is over: the holidays have begun.[15] The dream is ended: this is the morning" (*LB* 183).

The creative skill here is impressive. Viewpoint characters usually experience things directly and provide the perspective from which they are told; that poses the difficulty in depicting the deaths of viewpoint characters with which this paper began. Lewis, by having Aslan tell about the train wreck, has found a way to have the deaths of the viewpoint characters described to themselves in narrative form. And what they are told about is long since past. They are already on the other side of death, have gone through it, without pain or terror. The reality of death gives way to a greater Reality beyond it. As impressive as the narrative skill is the way that skill is used to present death as a factual reality, something to be accepted, not feared, but once again stripped of its emotional reality.

In *Till We Have Faces: A Myth Retold*, Lewis achieves the even more extraordinary feat of presenting the death of the first-person narrator (not just a central perspective character). In the last sentence of the story, the writer dies, in a way that adds to the reality of the fiction rather than undercutting it. We virtually see, or experience, the pen fall from her fingers as she passes away:

> I ended my first book with the words *No answer*. I know now, Lord, why you utter no answer. You are yourself the answer. Before your face questions die away. What other answer would suffice? Only words, words; to be led out to battle against other words. Long did I hate you, long did I fear you. I might—
>
> (I, Arnom, priest of Aphrodite, saved this roll and put it in the temple. From the other markings after the word *might*, we think the Queen's head must have fallen forward on them as she died and we cannot read them. ...)[16]

The ending is anticipated by the opening pages of the novel, where Orual describes the preparations for her death:

> I am old now and have not much to fear from the anger of gods.... My body, this lean carrion that still has to be washed and fed and have clothes hung about it daily with so many

changes, they may kill as soon as they please. The succession is provided for. My crown passes to my nephew (*TWHF* 3).

But we forget these foreshadowings as she moves smoothly into and through the narrative of her life; we then follow her back to the beginning, which is the ending.

At the end of the novel we experience the death of the character through whom we have been told the story; but we are prepared for that death by the deaths of many other characters (of Orual's mother, her stepmother, her father, the Old Priest, the first enemy she killed, the Fox, Bardia, and many others), but especially by the sacrifice of Psyche to end a famine and plague. Sacrifice normally involves the death of the victim, and that presumably is the case here, handled as in *The Last Battle* through symbols: Psyche is left on the sacred mountain as a sacrifice to the Shadowbrute, the son of Ungit, and is next seen in the land of the gods, across a river (a traditional symbol of death). Psyche assumes that being a sacrificial victim means death:

> "I see," said Psyche in a low voice. "You think it [the Brute] devours the offering. I mostly think so myself. Anyway, it means death. Orual, you didn't think I was such a child as not to know that? How can I be the ransom for all Glome unless I die? And if I am to go to the god, of course it must be through death" (*TWHF* 72).

Psyche perfectly exemplifies acceptance of death as a factual reality; she even welcomes death, had always experienced a kind of longing for death: "because it [the Grey Mountain] was so beautiful, it set me longing, always longing. Somewhere else there must be more of it. Everything seemed to be saying, Psyche come! But I couldn't (not yet) come and I didn't know where I was to come to. It almost hurt me. I felt like a bird in a cage when the other birds of its kind are flying home" (*TWHF* 74). Lewis develops in the book the theme of *Sehnsucht* which, as *Surprised by Joy* shows, played a crucial part in his own reconversion; and he develops the theme of sacrifice, of "accepted death," which he first explored in *The Problem of Pain*. "Martyrdom," he writes there, "always remains the supreme enacting and perfection of Christianity." But this doctrine of death is not peculiar to Christianity:

Nature herself has written it large across the world in the repeated drama of the buried seed and the re-arising corn. From nature, perhaps, the oldest agricultural communities learned it and with animal, or human, sacrifices showed forth for centuries the truth that "without shedding of blood is no remission"[17]. ... The Indian ascetic, mortifying his body on a bed of spikes, preaches the same lesson; the Greek philosopher tells us that the life of wisdom is "a practice of death." ... We cannot escape the doctrine by ceasing to be Christians. It is an "eternal gospel" revealed to men wherever men have sought, or endured, the truth: it is the very nerve of redemption, which anatomising wisdom at all times and in all places lays bare; the inescapable knowledge which the Light that lighteneth every man presses down upon the minds of all who seriously question what the universe is "about." The peculiarity of the Christian faith is not to teach this doctrine but to render it, in various ways, more tolerable.[18]

Till We Have Faces, though preChristian in setting, is Christian as it helps render that doctrine more tolerable, both through Psyche's eager embracing of sacrifice and Orual's reluctant, resistant acceptance of it. The voice of the god tells Orual, "Die before you die," and slowly, gradually she learns what that means. She must die to self—to her self-centeredness, her jealousy, her possessiveness—in order to find and accept her true self and gain salvation. In our eagerness for Orual to die to self and be spiritually reborn, we are prepared as well for her physical death, which comes, at the end of the book, not as tragedy but as triumph, not death as emotional reality but death as factual reality in its most fully positive and meaningful sense.

As Lewis described death in his nonfictional works, and depicted it in his fiction, the repeated refrain is that death is to be accepted, collectedly and nonemotionally, as a factual reality. Initially that unemotional acceptance is based on Lewis's Hamiltonianism, his determination to embrace the cool reserve he saw as marking his mother and her forebears, in contrast to his father's passion and lack of control. After his reconversion, when he comes to regard "accepted death" as at the heart of Christianity, the need for emotional reserve may have seemed all the more necessary in order to demonstrate his belief in the doctrine of "dying into life." Through the first three of the four most significant deaths he faced (his mother, his father, Charles Williams[19]), he maintained his determination not to reveal his feelings to the public. Only with the fourth, the death of his wife, does that determination change. In *A Grief Observed* Lewis does write about death as an emotional reality, as well as a factual reality; there he finally escapes the Hamiltonian persona that marks his earlier writings about death and shows himself as most fully human and vulnerable; and there he becomes most helpful to others as they face their own sorrows, no more able than he to encounter death solely as factual reality, without conceding its emotional reality as well.

PETER J. SCHAKEL

Peter J. Schakel received his B.A. from Central College in Iowa and his Ph.D. from the University of Wisconsin-Madison. He has taught at Hope College in Holland, Michigan, since 1969 and for the past twenty years has been the Peter C. and Emajean Cook Professor of English. He has written or edited six books on C.S. Lewis, including *Reading with the Heart: The Way into Narnia* (1979; on-line at http://hope.edu/academic/english/schakel/readingwiththeheart), *Reason and Imagination in C.S. Lewis: A Study of* **Till We Have Faces** (1984; on-line at http://hope.edu/academic/english/schakel/tillwehavefaces), *Imagination and the Arts in C.S. Lewis* (University of Missouri Press, 2002), and *The Way into Narnia: A Reader's Guide* (Wm. B. Eerdmans, 2005).

END NOTES

1. Margaret Anne Doody, "Death and the Novel," the James L. Clifford lecture at the meeting of the American Society for Eighteenth Century Studies, University of Notre Dame, April 3, 1998.

2. C.S. Lewis, *Surprised by Joy: The Shape of My Early Life* (New York: NY: Harcourt Brace & World), p. 18.

3. George Sayer, *C.S. Lewis and His Times* (San Francisco, CA: Harper & Row), pp. 133-134.

4. It is a generally non-emotional account, dwelling on the positive episodes in an admittedly dreadful situation. Don King argues persuasively that despite Lewis's later dismissal of the war as a time of "Guns and Good Company," it did in fact impact him deeply "C.S. Lewis's *Spirits in Bondage:* World War I Poet as Frustrated Dualist," *Christian Scholar's Review* 27:4, Summer 1998, pp. 454-58.

5. In a similar vein is his claim "that I have, almost all my life, been quite unable to feel that horror of nonentity, of annihilation, which, say, Dr. Johnson felt so strongly" (SJ 117).

6. David C. Downing, *Planets in Peril: A Critical Study of C.S. Lewis's Ransom Trilogy* (Amherst, MA: University of Massachusetts Press, 1992), pp. 11-12.

7. C.S. Lewis, "On Living in an Atomic Age," *Present Concerns: Essays by C.S. Lewis,* Walter Hooper, Ed. (San Diego, CA: Harcourt Brace Jovanovich, 1986), p. 73.

8. C.S. Lewis, "Cross-Examination," *God in the Dock: Essays on Theology and Ethics,* Walter Hooper, Ed. (Grand Rapids, MI: William B. Eerdmans, 1970), p. 266.

9. C.S. Lewis, *Out of the Silent Planet* (New York: NY: Macmillan, 1965), p. 140.

10. C.S. Lewis, *That Hideous Strength: A Modern Fairy-Tale for Grown-Ups* (New York: Macmillan, 1965), p. 368).

11. In looking back, there is an irony here. Ransom, in *That Hideous Strength*, comes to resemble Charles Williams, whom Lewis met in 1936 and came to regard as one of his closest friends. Williams wrote a number of fictional works, which influenced *That Hideous Strength* in form and style, and a large body of poetry reworking the Arthurian legends. The irony is that Williams, model for the Ransom who does not die, himself died very suddenly about two months before *That Hideous Strength* was published.

12. C.S. Lewis, *The Magician's Nephew* (New York, NY: Collier Books, 1970), p. 3.

13. J.R.R. Tolkien, "On Fairy-Stories," *Essays Presented to Charles Williams*, C.S. Lewis, Ed. (London: Oxford University Press, 1947), p. 81.

14. C.S. Lewis, *The Last Battle* (New York, NY: Collier, 1970), p. 128.

15. This sentence echoes Lewis's autobiography, with its death-as-factual-reality motif. In reflecting back on his experiences at his first, horrible, boarding school, run by a schoolmaster who was going insane, Lewis wrote: "the year was not all term. Life at a vile boarding school is in this way a good preparation for the Christian life, that it teaches one to live by hope. Even, in a sense, by faith; for at the beginning of each term, home and the holidays are so far off that it is as hard to realize them as to realize heaven. ... And yet, term after term, the unbelievable happened" (SJ, p. 26).

16. C.S. Lewis, *Till We Have Faces: A Myth Retold* (New York, NY: Harcourt, Brace & World, 1957), p. 308.

17. Hebrews 9:22.

18. C.S. Lewis, *The Problem of Pain* (New York, NY: Macmillan, 1962), pp. 103-104. See also "The Grand Miracle," *God in the Dock*, pp. 80-88, and *Miracles: A Preliminary Study* (Great Britain: Fontana Books, 1960), chapter 14.

19. The closest to a public expression of his emotion is the restrained poem "To Charles Williams," published in *Britain To-day* in August

1945, Poems, Walter Hooper, Ed. (London: Geoffrey Bles, 1964), p. 105. In the preface to *Essays Presnted to Charles Williams*, he called the experience of loss upon Williams's death "the greatest I have yet known" (p. xiv).

TOUCHSTONE OF REALITY: GREAT AWAKENINGS

By Michael A. Szuk

In 1942, C.S. Lewis wrote the following words through the pen of a senior tempter, Screwtape, to a junior tempter, Wormwood: "The characteristic of Pains and Pleasures is that they are unmistakably real, and therefore, as far as they go, give the man who feels them a touchstone of reality."[1] Lewis's theme of reality is clearly observed through pain and pleasure. This paper will survey his principle of the "Touchstone of Reality" in his fictional and non-fictional works and conclude with a synthesis and challenge to the modern reader.

While the phrase, "Touchstone of Reality" first appears in *The Screwtape Letters*, the theme of pleasure or pain and their relationship to reality predates itself in Lewis's mind. Indeed, most likely Lewis first met this truth in the writings of George MacDonald. Calling him, "my master; indeed I fancy I have never written a book in which I did not quote from him,"[2] Lewis provided his readers with a key to understanding the background to this concept. A generation earlier, Lewis had read these words from MacDonald: "The working out of this our salvation must be pain, and the handling of it down to them that are below must ever be in pain; but the eternal form of the will of God in and for us, is intensity of bliss."[3] This would mark the beginning of his thoughts on reality, pleasure and pain. Nine years preceding the publication of *The Screwtape Letters*, Lewis wrote an allegorical account of his conversion and entitled it *The Pilgrim's Regress: An Allegorical Apology for Christianity, Reason and Romanticism*. The touchstone theme is already present, although under a different name. Nevertheless its function is identical to that mentioned in *Screwtape*, namely, that genuine pleasure and pain, inherent in their nature, clear one's mind from nonsense and unreality. Pilgrim John learns from Father that "You must fear thrills, but you must not fear them too much. It is only a foretaste of that which the real Desirable will be when you have found it. ... First comes delight: then pain: then fruit. And then there is joy of the fruit, but that is different again from the fast delight."[4]

Lewis will specifically deal with the theme of pain as a touchstone of reality in *The Problem of Pain*. Written as an apologetic work, it predates *Screwtape* by two years. Again, we see how Lewis has maintained his philosophy of pain being the touchstone of reality. What is in fact interesting is that in both autobiography and in apologetic, Lewis found a comfortable medium by which to communicate truth. Here it is so clearly and so precisely defined that it finds its way in later writings as having been firmly established in his mind: "If the first and lowest operation of pain shatters the illusion that all is well, the second shatters the illusion that what we have, whether good or bad in itself, is our own and enough for us."[5] It is the concept of "unmasking evil" that comes out in *Screwtape* as a "Touchstone of Reality." Having highlighted some of the earlier works of Lewis's, the post-Screwtape development becomes even more significant and poignant. It is one thing to read an autobiography and feel the "intellectual" weight of Lewis's conclusions; moreover, his apologetics on pain and the goodness and omnipotence of God also carries a conspicuous distancing effect. But when Lewis set his principle into fictional accounts, the reader is struck with a sharp arrow that seldom misses its mark.

In *The Great Divorce: A Dream*, Lewis as the narrator is transported from a grey city of the afterlife to the outskirts of heaven. In one particularly sobering scene a woman ghost is distressed by her apparent nakedness and all of its preternatural concomitants. Filled with shame she asks why humans were born. The Spirit guide sent to accompany her on the way to the mountains replies, "For infinite happiness." This is very crucial to the remainder of the scene. She refuses to hear what the Spirit is saying to her, and finally " 'Then only one expedient remains,' said the Spirit, and to my great surprise he set a horn to his lips and blew ... A herd of unicorns came thundering through the glades. ... I heard the Ghost scream, and I think it made a bolt away from the bushes."[6] For Lewis, touchstones of reality are used to shake humans out of complacency, out of ruts, out of the quagmire of their own delusions. Indeed, as William Blake called it, "the mind-forged manacles" which trap humanity in the charnel pit of delusion.

In *Till We Have Faces: A Myth Retold*, Lewis brilliantly moves into the heart of the issue of possessive love. Throughout the entire novel, Orual suffers deeper and deeper losses, both externally and internally. Her pain, in this final instance, comes as a result of why the gods have not answered her, comes at the climax and sublimely shakes the reader into an epiphany of reality: "For suffering, it seems, is infinite, and our capacity without limit.... But things that many see may have no taste or moment in them at all, and things that are shown only to one may be spears and waterspouts of truth from the very depth of truth."[7] Clearly Lewis is demonstrating the touchstone of truth in synonymous language, replacing suffering for pain and truth for reality; nevertheless, the fact still remains that Orual comes to self-realization only through the touchstones of reality in her life. All along pains, and some pleasures, have been shouting out to her and in the end the mask of delusion falls away.[8]

Probably the most moving and the most graphic scene where Lewis demonstrates that pain awakes people from diabolical stupors is in *The Silver Chair*. The Green Witch, having enslaved Prince Rilian, Eustace, Jill and Puddleglum, attempts to twist and warp their views of reality. Puddleglum sticks his bare, webbed foot into the fire in order to clear his head. Lewis writes, "the pain itself made Puddleglum's head for a moment perfectly clear and he knew exactly what he really thought. There is nothing like a good shock of pain for dissolving certain kinds of magic."[9]

In conclusion, the theme of the Touchstone of Reality was present in Lewis's thought and writing from very early on up until the end of his life. More specifically, from his reading of George MacDonald, from *The Pilgrim's Regress* in 1933 to *A Grief Observed* in 1961 it encompasses his whole writing career. Furthermore, this theme not only spans his literary life time, it also transcends genre—from allegory (*The Pilgrim's Regress*), to fantasy (*Perelandra: Voyage to Venus*, *The Great Divorce*), to children's novels (*The Silver Chair*) and adult novels (*Till We Have Faces*), to his non-fictional writings (*The Problem of Pain*, *The Weight of Glory and Other Addresses*, *Transposition and Other Addresses*, *A Grief Observed*). Therefore, throughout his literary corpus, Lewis maintains that *reality*, truth in its unadulterated form, is mediated to sinful humanity through touchstones of reality. May we all escape Screwtape's specious and mind-dimming snares.

MICHAEL A. SZUK

Michael A. Szuk graduated in 2002 from Regent College, Vancouver, British Columbia, with his Master's degree in Christian studies and currently is working towards his Ph.D. in New Testament studies from the University of Wales (Bangor). While at Regent College, Michael studied literature and writing courses with Madeleine L'Engle, Earl Palmer and Mary Ellen Ashcroft. He has written several book reviews in *The Canadian C.S. Lewis Journal*, as well as two full-length articles—one on C.S. Lewis and one on J.R.R. Tolkien. Michael worked closely with Roger Stronstad, the last editor of *The Canadian C.S. Lewis Journal*. Michael is Registrar at Columbia Bible College, Abbotsford, British Columbia, and teaches in the area of New Testament, as well as a course on Modern Christian Literature. His literature studies have included the works of George MacDonald, G.K. Chesterton, C.S. Lewis, Dorothy L. Sayers, Charles Williams, J.R.R. Tolkien and Madeleine L'Engle.

END NOTES

1. C.S. Lewis, *The Screwtape Letters*. London: Geoffrey Bles, 1942, p. 67.

2. C.S. Lewis (ed.), *George MacDonald: 365 Readings*. New York, NY: Macmillan, 1947, p. xxxii.

3. Ibid., p. 76. Lewis found the source of this quote in George MacDonald's *Unspoken Sermons (Series Three)*. London: Longmans, Green and Co., 1891.

4. C.S. Lewis, *The Pilgrim's Regress: An Allegorical Apology for Christianity, Reason and Romanticism*. London: Geoffrey Bles, 1933, pp. 161-62. Here, in more philosophical terms, Lewis deals with both aspects of pain and pleasure. What is fascinating is that in *The Pilgrim's Regress* Lewis connects this with his concept of Joy (=*Sensucht*). Unfortunately the late Kathryn Lindskoog, in her otherwise excellent guidebook, *Finding the Landlord: A Guidebook to C.S. Lewis's Pilgrim's Regress* (Chicago, IL: Cornerstone Press, 1995, p. 91), misses this very key theme and focuses upon "the source and fruit of desire" rather than the predominant issue of pleasure and pain and how they relate to joy.

5. C.S. Lewis, *The Problem of Pain*. London: Geoffrey Bles, 1940, p. 83. This statement follows right on the heels of Lewis's oft quoted phrase, "God whispers to us in our pleasures, speaks in our conscience, but shouts in our pains: it is His megaphone to rouse a deaf world" (p. 81). It is Lewis's contention that "The human spirit will not even begin to try to surrender self-will as long as all seems to be well with it. Now error and sin both have this property, that the deeper they are the less their victim suspects their existence; they are masked evil" (p. 80).

6. C.S. Lewis, *The Great Divorce: A Dream*. New York, NY: Macmillan, 1946, pp. 57-58. George Musacchio, in his article, "Frightened by Unicorns: The Narrator of *The Great Divorce*," in *The Canadian C.S. Lewis Journal* (No. 88, Autumn 1995), pp. 15-18, and reprinted in the present book, calls this touchstone of reality a "divine arsenal":

"Apparently, fear has its place in the divine arsenal" (p. 17). What Lewis later explains is that the call of the unicorns was meant to frighten the woman into salvation. This is a very interesting usage in Lewis regarding fear (=pain) as a touchstone of reality.

7. C.S. Lewis, *Till We Have Faces: A Myth Retold*. London: Geoffrey Bles, 1956, p. 288. What is very curious is that in the literary criticism of *Till We Have Faces* rarely do commentators note the fact of the Touchstone theme, nor its critical role in the myth!

8. It is interesting to note that Lewis's original title was *Bareface* which has even greater significance than what Jocelyn Gibb, Bles's editor, finally chose. See George Sayer, *Jack: C.S. Lewis and His Times*. San Francisco, CA: Harper & Row, 1988, p. 234.

9. C.S. Lewis, *The Silver Chair*. London: Geoffrey Bles, 1953, p. 163.

THE AGONY AND THE ECSTASY OF C.S. LEWIS

By Walter Unger

"[It was] a short episode, of glory and tragedy."

W.H. Lewis, re Jack's life with Joy[1]

The life of C.S. Lewis, particularly the bittersweet thirteen years prior to his death on November 22, 1963, provides many provocative insights into the joys and sorrows of human existence. These insights come because of the vulnerability and integrity with which Lewis lived his life.

One would be hard pressed to find a more scrupulously honest account of the questions, doubts and fears involved in the grieving process than one sees in *A Grief Observed*. On the other hand, few authors have so graphically portrayed the process of extracting out of life its pleasures without resting in them as ends or mistaking them for the "settled happiness" which is to be found in God alone.

C.S. Lewis demonstrated through his life and writing that Christianity is not merely a "warm, fuzzy theology," as one critic of *Shadowlands* complained. It realistically addresses both the agony and the ecstasy of life.

Although Lewis had been wounded in his tour of service during World War I, he had not experienced a great deal of physical pain in the first half of his life. This is undoubtedly one of the chief factors for the humility he expresses in the preface to his *The Problem of Pain*, a book he at first wanted to write anonymously. He never boasted great fortitude and patience in the face of pain; indeed, quite to the opposite, he admits, "I have never for one moment been in a state of mind to which even the imagination of serious pain was less than intolerable."[2]

As he grew older, Lewis's body, which he likened to an old automobile, began to wear out. He was a chain smoker and loved his ale. He really did not take very good care of himself and found it difficult to live on the diet set for him. He was given to overwork and frequently suffered from exhaustion. In his fifties, he began to suffer from osteoporosis. Stepson Douglas Gresham believes Lewis not only neglected his health, but that he received inadequate medical help for his diseased prostate.[3]

Then there was the strain put on Lewis through Mrs. Janie King ("Minto") Moore's illness and brother Warnie's alcoholism. Lewis had agreed to care for Moore, mother of his war-time fallen comrade, "Paddy," and true to his word, he did so for thirty years. In her later years, Mrs. Moore was particularly demanding. Lewis was exceedingly charitable towards her. By 1950, she was rapidly showing signs of senility and had to be institutionalized. Lewis visited her every day. After his July 28, 1950, visit, he wrote to a friend: "She was for many years of a worrying and, to speak frankly, a jealous, exacting, and angry disposition." However, he added that "she now gets gentler—I dare to hope not only through weakness."[4]

After her son Paddy's death, Mrs. Moore had become an atheist. She chided Lewis and Warren for participating in Communion, which she called a "blood feast." It must have been one of the major disappointments of Lewis's life that Mrs. Moore, living under the same roof of one who was fast becoming the chief Christian apologist of the century, seemed so unmoved by Christianity. William Griffin writes:

> Monthly, sometimes even weekly, [Lewis] got news from
> correspondents who had been moved by his books or broadcasts

to undergo the conversion experience. Though he lived with Minto for thirty years, did housework, washed dishes, took the dog for a trot, all the while talking with her about one thing or another, he seemed not to have touched her soul.[5]

Lewis was reticent to discuss his own suffering. At age fifty, after he had come down with a severe streptococcus infection and had to be hospitalized, his doctor ordered a long vacation to restore his run-down body, but Lewis could not follow through since he had to watch over Warnie who was given to long bouts of drinking. A disappointed Lewis wrote to friend Arthur Greeves about this failed rest opportunity: "It wd. be better that the door of my prison had never been opened than if it now bangs in my face! How hard to submit to God's will."[6] George Sayer states that this was almost the only clear expression of the strain under which Lewis was then living and that he rarely discussed his exhaustion from overwork, his bad health, or his worry about Mrs. Moore and Warnie.[7]

LOVE AND LOSS

If there were ripples on the surface of C.S. Lewis's life up to 1951, what was to follow in his remaining years might be described as tumultuous, while at the same time glorious. These were the years of love and loss, agony and ecstasy. Stepson Douglas Greham speaks of Jack and Joy climbing from the depths of despair, building happiness from the ashes of promise, reaching the pinnacle of that happiness and then descending again, particularly Jack, to the very deepest pit of despair.[8]

Helen Joy Davidman began corresponding with C.S. Lewis in January 1950. It is fascinating to trace the evolution of a mere "academic" relationship to friendship, then romance, and finally love and Christian marriage. It is a bittersweet story from start to finish. Joy's illness with cancer intensified Jack's affection for her and from this time on he became aware of loving her. He wrote to a friend: "Never have I loved her more than since she was struck down."[9] The April 23, 1956, civil marriage was followed by a March 21, 1957, Christian marriage in the stark setting of a hospital ward. This was, in both Jack and Joy's full cognizance, a deathbed marriage. Nevertheless, Jack told

Joy they must not give way to utter hopelessness. Rather, he said "uncertainty is what God has given us for a cross."[10]

"As you may imagine," Lewis wrote to a friend, "new beauty and new tragedy have entered my life."[11]

To another he wrote, "I can hardly describe to you the state of mind I live in at present—except that all emotion, with me, is periodically drowned in sheer tiredness, [and] deep lakes of stupor. ..."[12]

With Joy's remission the couple experienced the glorious breadth of married love. Lewis wrote to correspondents that he never expected to have, in his sixties, the happiness that passed him by in his twenties.[13] In recalling this period, Lewis wrote in A Grief Observed:

> For those few years H. and I feasted on love; every mode of it—solemn and merry, romantic and realistic, sometimes as dramatic as a thunderstorm, sometimes as comfortable and unemphatic as putting on your soft slippers. No cranny of heart or body remained unsatisfied.[14]

The real agony of life after Joy is chronicled in A Grief Observed. In this book, as in his 1940 work, Lewis does not solve the problem of pain. That is inscrutable. What A Grief Observed and The Problem of Pain provide are complementary views—the latter the philosophical and theological; the former the gut-wrenching, experiential side of suffering. The Problem of Pain lays a foundation upon which to rebuild after the chaos of suffering and pain has taken away the emotional and intellectual strength to see beyond one's immediate grief. A person doesn't see things very clearly when his or her eyes are full of tears. The heart needs answers which go beyond what the mind provides. The battle with suffering and grief is profoundly internal, "a war waged not in textbooks but in the heart. Victory—if there will be victory—belongs ultimately to the spirit and not to reason alone."[15]

While in the midst of his grief over Joy's death, Lewis calls into question all the reasoned answers and cool theology of his earlier writings. He eventually reaffirms those basic beliefs but in a deeper and more profound way.

In *A Grief Observed*, Lewis asks questions good Christians are not supposed to ask, and if they do, people think there is something fundamentally wrong with their faith. One is simply supposed to believe.

Lewis reminds us that it is hard to believe what you cannot feel. He doubted the beneficence of God because, when in the depths of despair he approached God, he found a door slammed in his face and "a sound of bolting and double bolting on the inside. And after that, silence."[16]

Out of this sense of being totally forsaken came other dreadful feelings; he uses words such as "stunned," "concussed," "fear" and "guilt." "Why am I so afraid?" he asks. "Why do I feel guilty? Where is God in all of this?"

There is fear that Joy is not in the presence of God, but suffering more in purgatory or fear that she is extinct. "Can I honestly say that she is now anything?"[17]

Lewis speaks of coming to believe such dreadful things about God— that He is evil, a Cosmic Sadist, an Eternal Vivisector, a Spiteful Imbecile. God creates a noble hunger for love and connectedness, and as in his case it was "long unsatisfied, [but] met at last its proper food, and almost instantly the food was snatched away. Fate (or whatever it is) delights to produce a great capacity and then frustrate it. Beethoven went deaf. By your standards a mean joke; the monkey trick of a spiteful imbecile."[18]

Lewis's faith seems to have collapsed like a house of cards. The comfort of friends is rebuffed with a "don't come talking to me about the consolations of religion or I shall suspect that you don't understand."[19] Even the comfort of Scripture doesn't seem to apply to him, the words "so obviously addressed to ... betters."[20]

About halfway through *A Grief Observed* Lewis began to call himself to task for his hideous thoughts, for telling God what he thought of Him. "And of course," he writes, "as in all abusive language, 'what I thought' didn't meant what I thought true."[21] He then begins to rebuild and write about a restoration of faith. He confesses: "I have gradually been coming to feel that the door is no longer shut and bolted. Was it my own frantic need that slammed it in my face?"[22] A little later he writes: "God has not been trying an experiment on my faith or love in order to find out their quality. He knew it already. It was I who didn't."[23]

What seems to finally bring a sense of resolution to Lewis is a reaffirmation of the hope of Heaven. Through the eyes of a renewed faith, he sees Joy in God's hand. "I think of her as a sword," he writes. "Perhaps the earthly life I shared with her was only part of the tempering. Now perhaps He grasps the hilt, weighs the new weapon, makes lightnings with it in the air. A right Jerusalem blade."[24]

Lewis seeks to be ruthlessly honest about his motives. He desperately wants to keep God Himself as the centre of his focus and worship, not Joy. And so he asks:

> Am I, for instance, just sidling back to God because I know that if there's any road to H., it runs through Him? But then of course I know perfectly well that He can't be used as a road. If you're approaching Him not as the goal but as a road, not as the end but as a means, you're really not approaching Him at all.[25]

A little later, he calls himself to get on with the highest duty he has. "I know the two great commandments, and I'd better get on with them."[26]

The last three years of Lewis's life were a continued intermingling of grief with the joy of Christian hope. "He overcame his grief," writes Douglas Gresham, "to the extent that he could function again as a human being and as a writer—but there was never, ever, any time at which he wasn't conscious of his loss."[27]

Lewis's already poor health rapidly deteriorated. A diseased prostate, with complications spreading to his kidneys and heart, finally took him on November 22, 1963. Good friend Austin Farrer observed:

"The life Lewis had lived with zest, he surrendered with composure. He was put almost beside himself by his wife's death; he seemed easy at the approach of his own."[28] Two days before his passing, Lewis said to

Warnie, "I have done all that I was sent into the world to do, and I am ready to go."[29]

Reflecting on the agony and the ecstasy of C.S. Lewis helps us put the man in proper perspective. He was not a perfect Christian. Yes, by New Testament teaching he was a saint, as are all believers, but not a plaster saint.

Perhaps we should simply see Lewis as a transparent, vulnerable fellow pilgrim—a voice crying in the wilderness of the love and the loss of this world:

> Remember, these are, after all, Shadowlands. Real life has not yet begun. Go further up and further in. Before you know it, you will be through the gate. You will then begin Chapter One of the Great Story in which there is only ecstasy and in which each chapter is better than the one before.

WALTER UNGER

Walter Unger became a C.S. Lewis fan midway in his academic career. Reading *Mere Christianity*, then the Chronicles of Narnia, to his children was a start. Using C.S. Lewis in his Religious Classics course brought Lewis's genius to hundreds of his students at Columbia Bible College, Abbotsford, British Columbia.

Walter was honoured to be asked to be a tutor at the first C.S. Lewis Summer Institute held in Oxford, England, in 1988. He attended two more Institutes, including the 1998 Lewis Centennial Celebration.

Walter and his wife, Laura, had the privilege of hosting C.S. Lewis's stepson, Douglas Gresham, in their home during his 1993 British

Columbia lecture tour. In 1997 Walter and Laura visited Douglas and Merrie at their beautiful manor in Leighlinbridge, County Carlow, Ireland.

Walter studied at Mennonite Brethren Bible College (B.R.E., 1959), Hamilton Teacher's College (1960), University of Waterloo (B.A., 1964), Trinity Evangelical Divinity School (M.A. in The History of Christian Thought, 1969), and Simon Fraser University (Ph.D. in American Intellectual History, 1982). He has also done post-doctoral studies at Regent's Park College, Oxford (1985). He was a public school teacher (1954-56; 1960-68); Assistant Pastor, Fairview Mennonite Brethren Church (1965-68); and instructor at Mennonite Brethren Bible Institute (1969-70).

He has been a prolific writer. His articles have appeared in more than twenty periodicals and journals. He is President Emeritus of Columbia Bible College where he has served continuously since 1969 (Faculty, 1970-), (Academic Dean, 1970-78; 1980-85), and (President, 1978-80, 1985-2001). He is now President Emeritus.

END NOTES

1. As cited in Brian Sibley, C.S. Lewis Through the Shadowlands: The Story of His life With Joy Davidman (Grand Rapids, MI: Fleming H. Revell, 1994), p. 157.

2. C.S. Lewis, The Problem of Pain (London and Glasgow: Collins, 1966), p. vii. Lewis began writing The Problem of Pain in 1939. The book was first published in 1940.

3. Douglas H. Gresham, Lenten Lands: My childhood with Joy Davidman and C.S. Lewis (London: Collins, 1989), p. 134.

4. As cited in William Griffin, Clive Staples Lewis A Dramatic Life (San Franciosco: Harper & Row, Publishers, 1986), p. 310.

5. Ibid., p. 317.

6. As cited in George Sayer, *Jack: C.S. Lewis and His Times* (San Francisco: Harper & Row, Publishers, 1988), p. 200-201.

7. *Ibid.*, p. 201.

8. Gresham, *Lenten Lands*, p. 122.

9. As cited in Sayer, *Jack*, p. 222.

10. As cited in Sibley, *C.S. Lewis*, p. 131.

11. *Ibid.*, p. 127.

12. *Ibid.*

13. Griffin, *Clive Staples Lewis*, p. 396.

14. C.S. Lewis, *A Grief Observed* (New York: Bantam Books, 1976), p. 6-7.

15. Robert Walter Wall, "The Problem of Observed Pain: A Study of C.S. Lewis on Suffering," *Journal of the Evangelical Theological Society* 26 (1983), p. 444.

16. Lewis, *A Grief Observed*, p. 4.

17. *Ibid.*, p. 24.

18. *Ibid.*, p. 19.

19. *Ibid.*, p. 28.

20. *Ibid.*, p. 29.

21. *Ibid.*, p. 46.

22. *Ibid.*, p. 53.

23. *Ibid.*, p. 61.

24. *Ibid.*, p. 73.

25. *Ibid.*, p. 79.

26. *Ibid.*, p. 81.

27. Cited in Sibley, *C.S. Lewis*, p. 167.

28. Cited in *ibid.*, p. 178.

29. Cited in Griffin, *Clive Staples Lewis*, p. 447.

VISITING C.S. LEWIS'S OXFORD

By Diane Vint

It was my first visit to Oxford and I'd been anticipating the trip since January when Roger and Laurel Stronstad first asked me if I'd like to accompany them. Of special interest to me was the fact that C.S. Lewis spent so many years of his life in and around Oxford and I was traveling with two people who were able to arrange for me to see all the related points of interest. I was not disappointed. My interest in C.S. Lewis stems from the time at age nine when my grade three teacher introduced me to *The Lion, the Witch and the Wardrobe* and it has increased ever since.

We spent the entire morning of our first day in Oxford on a C.S. Lewis/J.R.R. Tolkien tour with Peter Cousin. Peter is a taxi driver in Oxford who became interested in Lewis some years ago after picking up a fare who wanted to trace some of Lewis's steps. Since that day Peter has researched and become familiar with all points of interest in regards to Lewis, and others of the Inklings, in and around Oxford.

We began by visiting most of the houses that C.S. Lewis lived in, from the house at 1 Mansfield Road where he roomed in December 1916 when he came up to Oxford to write his university entrance exams, through all the homes that he and Mrs. Janie King Moore rented together and the house where Joy Davidman lived when she first came to Oxford, right up to the Kilns. We were unable to go into any of the homes except for the Kilns, because they are all private residences. So we merely took pictures. The majority of the homes were of the traditional brick variety found throughout Oxford, varying in size and in the size of the gardens.

After we viewed all of these houses, plus some of the Tolkien family homes, Peter drove us to Holy Trinity Church in Headington, where Lewis attended. The church was open when we arrived, so we were able to go inside. After Peter introduced us to the rector we looked around. There is a plaque commemorating the exact place in the pew where Lewis always sat, which, oddly enough, was directly behind a stone pillar which blocked the entire view of the front of the church. In place of one of the stained glass windows there is an etched glass window depicting various characters and scenes from the Narnia Chronicles. It was beautiful to see the light coming through and illuminating Aslan, Digory riding Fledge, and the Dawn Treader, to name just a few of the characters and scenes.

After spending some time inside the church Peter led us out to the graveyard. Holy Trinity Church is beautifully situated and looking back at it from the graveyard was breathtaking. It is a 150-year-old stone church surrounded by flowers and trees. C.S. Lewis, Warnie Lewis and Mrs. Moore are all buried in the graveyard and after we had paid our respects to each, we turned our faces towards the Kilns.

I had not expected to be able to go inside of the Kilns, but Peter, as resourceful as ever, phoned ahead and made arrangements. As we drove towards the Kilns I kept expecting to leave the town behind and head out into the countryside, having preconceived ideas from the film *Shadowlands*. I was greatly surprised, therefore, to see the house at the end of a cul-de-sac surrounded by other houses and no pond in immediate sight! The beautiful gardens and the house itself soon dispelled any small disappointment. We entered and were immediately ushered into the common room. The C.S. Lewis Foundation has restored the house to its original plan and furnished it as closely as possible to how Lewis would have furnished it. In the common room we were given a brief history of the house and then taken on a tour, consisting of Lewis's study, bedroom and the dining room. In the dining room, on display, was Warnie Lewis's typewriter, which was used to type some of

C.S. Lewis's correspondence and some of Warnie's manuscripts. It is a far cry from today's laptop computers!

It was lunch time when we finished at the Kilns, so we piled back into Peter's taxi for a return trip to Oxford and to the Eagle and Child (a.k.a. the Bird and Baby) for lunch. The Inklings used to gather there every Tuesday morning in a tiny back room called the Rabbit Room. The room now contains photos of Charles Williams, J.R.R. Tolkien and C.S. Lewis, as well as plaques commemorating the Inklings. We found a table in the Rabbit Room and enjoyed a hearty lunch.

After lunch Peter had to leave us, and Roger, Laurel and I wandered up the block to the building that used to contain the registry office. It was here that C.S. Lewis married Joy Davidman in 1956.

Though the "formal" tour had ended that morning we were by no means done with Lewis's Oxford. Over the course of the next week we visited many other places which Lewis frequented. We went to Magdalen College one afternoon and toured the grounds. We saw the New Building where Lewis had his rooms and walked up Addison's Walk to view the plaque that had been put up in honour of Lewis's Centenary. On Sunday evening we attended Evensong at Magdalen College Chapel. We had attended church at the University Church of St. Mary the Virgin earlier that day. It was in this church that C.S. Lewis preached his famous wartime sermon, "The Weight of Glory." On our last day in Oxford we bussed out to the crematorium and viewed the commemorative plaque which Lewis placed there in honour of his wife, Joy. It seemed that everywhere we went in Oxford Roger was able to point out something relevant to C.S. Lewis.

Probably one of the biggest highlights for me, of our time in Oxford, was meeting Walter Hooper at the end of our visit. He invited us to his home for tea. It was an interesting experience and he is a wonderful man. I was fascinated to listen to him talk about C.S. Lewis and his brother Warnie. One thing in particular that he told us sticks out in my mind, probably because I had never heard it before. On Walter's wall there is a framed map of a little town in Italy called Narnia. It was from this town that Lewis took the name for the country of Narnia. The tomb of Blessed Lucy of Narnia (1476-1544 A.D.), a Dominican nun, is in Narnia. Walter was unsure if Lewis knew thus or if it was merely a coincidence that the heroine in *The Lion, the Witch and the Wardrobe* is named Lucy. Spending time with Walter was the perfect way to end our visit to Oxford.

Though Oxford is filled with places of interest in respect to a multitude of literary figures, many of whose writings I am familiar with, it was C.S. Lewis's Oxford that I was most eager to see and learn about. During the course of our stay C.S. Lewis, the man, came alive for me in a way he never had before, despite my reading so much of his work. The visit was an experience I'll never forget, and one that I hope will be repeated!

DIANE VINT

Diane Vint was born in Vancouver, British Columbia, and currently resides with her husband, Jakob, in Abbotsford, British Columbia. Diane graduated from Summit Pacific College (formerly Western Pentecostal Bible College), Abbotsford, British Columbia, in 1993, with a Bachelor of Theology degree. Currently she is pursuing graduate studies at Regent College, Vancouver, British Columbia, on a part-time basis. Diane works at Summit Pacific College, where she has been employed since 1993, in Public Relations. In 2000 Diane traveled to England with Roger and Laurel Stronstad. At that time Roger was the editor of the now-defunct *Canadian C.S. Lewis Journal*. It is as a result of that trip that Diane wrote "Visiting C.S. Lewis's Oxford."

Testimonials

HOW I BECAME INTERESTED IN C.S. LEWIS

By Carolyn Keefe

In the fall of 1946 I matriculated at Oberlin College. I had never even heard of C.S. Lewis. Providentially, that lack in my life was soon to be remedied.

When I had applied for admission to Oberlin, I had known that in spite of its strong Christian heritage the school was no Wheaton. Its history as the first coeducational college in the United States and the first to admit Blacks on the same basis as whites was lauded on campus, but it was not the religious motivation that had produced these results. Under the influence of Oberlin's second president, the prominent nineteenth-century evangelist Charles G. Finney, and his associates, social action had been linked with the claims of the Gospel. But it never took the place of the Gospel. Around the turn of the century, however, as biblical higher criticism made its way into the classroom, the school's Christian foundation began to erode. I was not surprised by what I found in the late forties because my home church pastor had incessantly warned his congregation about the dangers of theological drift into skepticism and unbelief.

Inasmuch as I was a religion major and able to take classes in the graduate seminary as well as the college, I had ample opportunity to gain a close perspective on the prevailing religious ideas. Every religion professor I encountered presupposed a naturalistic basis for Christianity. Among the consequences of this starting point was the loss of biblical authority and the deity of Christ. Professors gave lengthy explanations (short on solid evidence) for why traditional datings of books could no longer be accepted, thus excluding revelation and predictive prophecy. Jesus was viewed, not as a Saviour from sin (in lectures the word *sin* was spoken only in ridicule), but as the Universal Good Example. The Sermon on the Mount, revered as no other portion of the New Testament, was read through rose coloured glasses, and the extraordinary demands of Jesus's Lordship were glibly overlooked. Love, justice, and mercy were hailed; humankind's perverseness and God's judgment were cast aside. I recognized these teachings as the currently popular Social Gospel. C.S. Lewis had already pronounced such beliefs "Christianity and water."

The very fall that I plunged into the challenging Oberlin waters, an Inter-Varsity Christian Fellowship chapter was chartered on campus. I immediately joined it. That early group numbering about twenty included representatives of the changing student population: five were World War II veterans and one was a Houghton College teacher who was pursuing an advanced degree in music. The veterans were not bullied by professors intent on upgrading their outmoded religious ideas, and the graduate student had something none of the rest of us had—a collection of C.S. Lewis books. These two conditions helped shape the group's outspoken Christian witness.

Soon after the chapter's formation we took advantage of a library privilege available to recognized campus organizations. We acquired an empty shelf in the stacks where we placed our own books for the use of others in the group. David Heydenburk, on leave from Houghton College, brought his copies of the three slim volumes that later (in 1952) were joined in Mere Christianity: The Case for Christianity, Christian Behaviour, Beyond Personality. Also from his stock came The Screwtape Letters.

Even today I can remember my excitement upon entering this special section of the library. Because David had already praised Lewis as an apologist, I sought out his works. As I perused them, the symbols from Lewis's pen commanded further attention, and, if I recall correctly, I first signed out *The Case for Christianity*. Standing in the quiet cave of books, I was engrossed by the rough and tumble of competing ideas, never guessing that the author I had just met would engage not only my personal but professional life.

As the Lewis books began to circulate among the Inter-Varsity members, what were the effects? For one thing, Lewis joined our arsenal of Christian scholars such as Robert Dick Wilson, J. Gresham Machen, Sir Frederic Kenyon, and F.F. Bruce who kept their beliefs and brains intact. Some of our professors scoffed at that possibility. In fact, an English professor chided one veteran that by the time he graduated he would not be a Christian. By pointing to Christian scholars of recognized brilliance, we refuted the outrageous claim that "no intellectuals still believe all that biblical nonsense."

More substantive outcomes of reading the Lewis books can be traced to content and form. Like Lewis, our group strove to present a non-denominational, mere Christian witness. We were not concerned about splitting theological hairs, so we did not let ourselves be drawn into disputes over matters such as mode of baptism and nature of the Eucharist. Lewis was instructive on separating major and minor issues and on knowing where Christian advocates had to take a stand. For faith to maintain its essential character, the supernatural could not be extricated. He was unequivocal about that. Lewis dealt with all the salient matters under attack and showed how without a life transformed by the living Triune God no genuine love was possible. We welcomed these reinforcements from the Oxford don and viewed our common stance as reclaiming the lost Oberlin religious tradition.

In form, Lewis's succinct, once-for-radio-talk treatments were ideal for verbal witness on campus. Our outreach took various communication modes—classroom challenge, spontaneous conversation, dorm "bull session," Bible study, and student-conducted Sunday worship. We often used Lewis's chain of argument, even his exact words, to make a point. Understandably, his "poached egg" dilemma concerning the deity of Christ was a favourite approach. Sometimes one of his phrases would be helpful. His catchy chapter title, "Nice People or New Men," gave entree to discussion about the biblical concept of human nature. Thus

Lewis entered our vocabulary and strategy of Christian witness, and even though the in-depth analyses of the other scholars in our arsenal were better suited for our research papers, no one could equal Lewis for lively oral rejoinders.

Almost fifty years have elapsed since the events just described, yet a commonality binds the decades. The veteran who graduated without losing his faith and I have collected long shelves of books by and about Lewis. And the Oberlin Inter-Varsity Christian Fellowship is thriving, and, as I am told, still finds C.S. Lewis a compelling co-apologist.

Carolyn Keefe

Carolyn Keefe, Professor Emerita of Communication Studies, West Chester (Pennsylvania) University, graduated from Oberin College with an A.B. in religion. When her daughter, Cheryl, and her son, Larry, were ten and eight years old, respectively, she started on her path to graduate school studies and earned an M.A. in rhetoric and public address from Temple University; an M.A. in religious studies from Villanova University; and an Ed.D. in educational leadership from the University of Pennsylvania.

During her career in higher education, first at Rutgers University (Camden branch) and then at West Chester University, she directed competitive speech and debate programs (forensics). She has edited and/or authored numerous articles, book reviews, poems and books, including *C.S. Lewis: Speaker and Teacher*; held major offices in professional organizations; and received significant teaching and service awards. Among her distinctions are the 1990 Pennsylvania Professor of the Year Award and two scholarships established at West Chester

University in her name. She also has lectured widely on C.S. Lewis and biblical topics.

Now a widow, Dr. Keefe was married for over fifty-five years to the Reverend Frederick L. Keefe, who served three Presbyterian churches in Pennsylvania, taught at Lincoln University and the Conwell School of Theology, and lectured in scores of churches and other venues. Currently, Dr. Keefe is a member of four boards, and she continues her long association with the national forensics honourary Pi Kappa Delta by serving as the sponsor of the WCU-PKD Alumni Chapter. That role keeps her in touch with her former speech and debate team members, as well as with the rising generation of intercollegiate competitors.

FROM G.K. CHESTERTON TO C.S. LEWIS

By *Peter Milward, S.J.*

I forget when I first made the acquaintance of C.S. Lewis; but it was, no doubt, owing to his *Screwtape Letters*, which I read while I was a boy at Wimbledon. Immediately on reading, I was transformed into a fan of his, and I was always pleased to hear his book quoted, as it was so often, in our school retreats. I was also envious of the boys at our sister school in North London, Stamford Hill, where I heard one of the Jesuit fathers was using the book as his textbook for Religious Doctrine classes, albeit by an Anglican author! Soon after war broke out, I went on to read his other best-seller, *The Problem of Pain*, and his radio talks on Christianity, then published separately as *Broadcast Talks*, *Right and Wrong: A Clue to the Meaning of the Universe* and *What Christians Believe*. A third and fourth series, *Christian Behaviour* and *Beyond Personality: Or First Steps In the Doctrine of the Trinity*, were only later added under the title of *Mere Christianity*.

It must have been my reading of these last-mentioned books that led me to relate my growing addiction to C.S. Lewis to my previous passion for G.K. Chesterton. Here was another great Christian author emerging as the leading champion of the faith in wartime England, the one on whom—for all his allegiance to another, Anglican denomination—Chesterton's mantle seemed to have fallen. It was only later, after my coming to Japan in 1954, that I learnt both from his autobiographical *Surprised by Joy: The Shape of My Early Life* and from his posthumous *God in the Dock: Essays on Theology and Ethics*, that Chesterton's writings had indeed been instrumental in his conversion from atheism to Christianity, above all *The Everlasting Man*.

My impression of Lewis's affinity with Chesterton was both deepened and enlarged when I went up to Oxford in 1950 as a Jesuit student to read the Classics. Soon after my arrival at Campion Hall for the Michaelmas Term we had a guest night to which Lewis himself had been invited by the Master, Fr. Tom Corbishley. My first impression on setting eyes on him was one of astonishment, since, for all his intellectual affinity with Chesterton, I had formed the image of Lewis as a slim, ascetic-looking man; yet here was a burly, red-faced, jovial man with an egg-head and a booming voice—and, as I later heard, no less fond of his pint of beer than of his tobacco pipe. After all, his affinity with Chesterton extended from the mind to the body, from a witty intellect to a corpulent frame, though he was more portly than fat.

From the beginning I made a point attending the meetings of the renowned Oxford University Socratic Club over which he presided in his genial, democratic manner, leaving Miss "Stella" Aldwinckle to take the chair. There I could observe him every week at closer quarters and listen to his occasional interventions in the discussion, when everything he said, though all too brief, was penetrating and to the point. For the most part, he seemed to be restraining himself under extreme provocation, till he could (like the Psalmist) keep silence no longer; and then his utterances, though deferential, could be devastating. In the same way, when I changed (on my appointment for Japan) from Classical Mods to English, I made a point of attending all the lectures of "Mr. Lewis," specifically his "prolegomena" to medieval and renaissance literature, which were subsequently published, the former under the title of *The Discarded Image: An Introduction to Medieval and Renaissance Literature* and the latter as the lengthy introduction, "Old Learning and New Ignorance," to his learned *English Literature in the Sixteenth Century, Excluding Drama*. These lectures were by far the most popular of all those provided by the School of English, since the content was so fascinating, the presentation was so lucid, and the delivery was so clear and considerate for note-taking students.

All this time, I had only watched and listened to Lewis from afar, as a distant admirer; but in my final year I summoned up the courage to ask him after his last lecture if I might come and see him in his rooms at Magdalen. I particularly wished to ask him about his evident interest in angels, which I had noticed in my favourite novel of his, *Out of the Silent Planet*, since I myself had a special interest in the angelology of St. Thomas. But when I visited him in his rooms at the appointed time, I was non-plussed by his opening question, "Why do you think so many Irishmen remain bachelors?" As I was thinking more of angels, it never occurred to me that this was a very personal question relating to himself as an Irishman and a bachelor. It was only long after my arrival in Japan that I came to realize how at that very time his thoughts were moving from angels in outer space to marriage with an American lady named Joy Davidman; and so when I first read his autobiography, *Surprised by Joy*, I had no inkling of the ambiguity in the title.

At the *viva* exam after my written finals in English, I found Lewis on the examining board; and it was he who opened proceedings with another question that left me non-plussed: "Would you tell us something about some minor eighteenth-century author you have read and enjoyed?" All I could say was, like Shakespeare's Cordelia, "Nothing"; and so I got off to a somewhat inauspicious start. The effect was soon counteracted when I got off to a better start for Japan, almost immediately after that *viva*, about the very time Lewis himself was starting for his new academic appointment at Magdalene College, Cambridge. Once I was in Japan, it wasn't long before I felt the prompting to renew my brief contact with Lewis by way of correspondence, first in connection with my ideas and his ideas on angels, and then with an article I was writing on his trilogy of science fiction. Thus there began between us a long, if fitful, correspondence, continuing till the very eve (if not the actual day) of his death, some items of which were published in the *Letters of C.S. Lewis*, while I sent the originals to the C.S. Lewis collection at Wheaton College, Illinois.

About this correspondence, the first thing that impressed me was the neatness and illegibility of Lewis's handwriting. His letters were a delight to look at, but a torment to decipher, till out of all the labour was born the joy of eventual enlightenment, reminding me of Christ's words about the sorrow and joy of a woman in childbirth. I felt the personality of Lewis himself in them, and I would not have had him type them for all the world! In quantity his letters were not so long— he must have had so many to write!—but in quality they were so pregnant with matter for reflection. He stated his thoughts simply and straightforwardly, even at times bluntly, as when he remarked of a certain famous Jesuit (in an unusually long letter), "I am entirely on the side of your Society for shutting de Chardin up." He could hardly have been called a Teilhardian! Another thing that impressed me about his letters was the way he invariably responded not only to my letters (even when no reply was called for) but even to my Japanese Christmas cards. He never sent me a Christmas card, as he apparently disliked the custom and (no doubt) the chore involved in this "commercialism" of Christmas, but he admired the Japanese picture of Bethlehem I had sent him, the work of the Carmelite sisters in Kyoto.

It was after my study of his science fiction that I turned to the Narnia stories for which he has since become so famous, not least here in Japan. They confirmed me in my esteem for his powers as well of lucid thought and exposition as of rich and original imagination. In one of his letters to me, apropos not of these stories but of J.R.R. Tolkien's *The Lord of the Rings*, he referred me to his friend and colleague's important essay on fairy stories in *Essays Presented to Charles Williams*. Following his reference, I came to realize how deeply indebted both he and Tolkien must have been, not so much to *The Everlasting Man*, with its Christian view of history, as to Chesterton's *Orthodoxy*, particularly its inspiring and seminal chapter on "The Ethics of Elfland" (which I find never fails to inspire my Japanese students from year to year). In a sense, his Narnia stories may be said to be an expression of Lewis's own elfland; and in so far as they point to a moral if not a Christian allegory (for all the odd reluctance of Lewis himself to admit the fact), it is to the ethics of Elfland.

Thus it was not only as a witty apologist for Christianity in his earlier writings, but also as a deeply imaginative Christian author in his later stories, that Lewis may be seen as having taken up the prophetic mantle of Chesterton in our time. He himself, as he told me, found these stories much more congenial to his temperament than his former *Screwtape Letters*, as a result of which his name had come to be all too closely associated in the minds of his readers with that of the devil! It was as if, thanks to Narnia, he had been purified of that hellish association and raised by the power of Aslan to that heaven which is reserved for those who (like Chesterton) have become as little children. And now, I find, he is not only (as we may hope) in heaven but also in the stained-glass windows of churches in America—such as one I myself came across at St. David's Episcopal Church in Denton, Texas. It is as if "C.S." has been transformed to "St."

PETER MILWARD, S.J.

Peter Milward is an English Jesuit who has been teaching in Japan, at Sophia University, Tokyo, for the past 50 years. He studied the Classics and English literature at Oxford from 1950 to 1954, and thus was taught by C.S. Lewis. After arriving in Japan, he engaged in a long correspondence with Lewis, which is soon to appear in Vol. III of the Collected Letters (ed., Walter Hooper). He is also founder of the G.K. Chesterton Society of Japan and co-founder of the C.S. Lewis Society of Japan (with K. Yamagata). He is the author of *A Challenge to C.S. Lewis* (1995).

Narnia

THE LION, THE WITCH AND THE WASTEBASKET: DISCARDED FRAGMENTS OF THE NARNIA CHRONICLES

By David C. Downing

As remarkable as they are in themselves, the Chronicles of Narnia are equally remarkable for the comparative ease with which they were created. Even while fulfilling his responsibilities as an Oxford don, and working steadily on *Surprised by Joy: The Shape of My Early Life* and *English Literature in the Sixteenth Century, Excluding Drama*, C.S. Lewis dashed off the first five Narnia Chronicles in less than three years between the summer of 1948 and the spring of 1951.

For most of the Chronicles, the main creative block seemed to come not in the stories themselves but in their titles. For two books, Lewis's working titles did indeed become the published titles when they were issued by Geoffrey Bles: *The Lion, the Witch and the Wardrobe* and *The Voyage of the "Dawn Treader."* The rest of the working titles, though, were subject to ongoing discussion and negotiation. *Prince Caspian* was originally "Drawn into Narnia" and then "A Horn in Narnia" (both referring to Susan's horn which called the Pevensie children to the rescue of Caspian). *The Horse and His Boy* might have been called "Narnia and the North" or "The Desert Road to Narnia" or "The Horse Stole the Boy." *The Silver Chair* was first "The Wild Waste Lands," then possibly "Night Under Narnia" or even "Gnomes Under Narnia." *The Magician's Nephew* was originally simply "Polly and Digory." *The Last*

Battle seemed less of a battle, with only one alternative title, "The Last Chronicle of Narnia" (Green and Hooper 243-248).

Apart from their titles, though, the whole world of Narnia unfolded in Lewis's imagination with impressive celerity. The last book in the series seemed to come as easily as the first five. Lewis seemed to have little trouble telling about the final days of his subcreated world, beginning *The Last Battle* in the autumn of 1952 and finishing it by the following spring.

It was a different story with *The Magician's Nephew*, the creation account of Narnia and the most intensely personal narrative in the series. Lewis took up this tale soon after completing *The Lion, the Witch and the Wardrobe*. But he did not finish it until all the other stories in the series were completed in the spring of 1954. All in all, Lewis completed six of the Narnia Chronicles in a five-year period, 1948-53; the seventh, *The Magician's Nephew*, seems by far the greatest creative challenge, with five years between its inception and completion (1949-54) and with two lengthy sections that were not used in the published version.

Of course, in saying the books were created in the years 1948 to 1954 is to speak of the writing process, not the creative process as a whole. Actually, one could argue that while the Chronicles were written at a pace of more than one per year, they were most of Lewis's lifetime in the making. In "It All Began with a Picture," Lewis himself explained that "the *Lion* all began with a picture of a Faun carrying an umbrella and parcels in a snowy wood. The picture had been in my mind since I was about sixteen. Then one day, when I was about forty, I said to myself, 'Let's try to make a story about it.'" (*Worlds* 53)

Actually, when he was "about forty," Lewis got only one paragraph into his first Narnian story and then set it aside for nearly a decade. At the beginning of the second world war in September 1939, Lewis's household at the Kilns accepted children who were evacuated from London during the Blitz. This seemed to give Lewis the premise for his story and so he began on an odd scrap of paper:

> This book is about four children whose names were Ann, Martin, Rose, and Peter. But it is most about Peter who was the youngest. They all had to go away from London suddenly because of the Air Raids, and because Father, who was in the Army, had gone off to the War and Mother was doing some kind of war work. They were sent to stay with a kind of relation of Mother's who was a very old Professor who lived all by himself in the country. (Green and Hooper 238)

That seems to be as far as Lewis got with his Narnia tales until he casually remarked to Chad Walsh in the summer of 1948 that he was hoping to complete a children's book he had begun "in the tradition of E. Nesbit" (Green and Hooper 238).

There has been no shortage of speculation about why a world-famous Christian apologist and literary critic nearing fifty would take up the humble genre of children's fiction. Humphrey Carpenter and A.N. Wilson have argued that Lewis was pummeled in a philosophical debate with the Wittgensteinian philosopher Elizabeth Anscombe in February 1948 and came away feeling that he could better express his Christian worldview in imaginative fiction than in intellectual disputation (Carpenter 216-222; Wilson 210-214). But Richard L. Purtill has all-but-refuted this thesis, showing that the famous debate was not nearly as one-sided as it is sometimes portrayed, and that Anscombe herself didn't think Lewis felt particularly traumatized by the encounter (Walker 45-53).

Another of Lewis's biographers, Roger Lancelyn Green, has given himself some of the credit, noting that his own foray into children's fiction, a manuscript called "The Wood that Time Forgot," seems to have stimulated Lewis's interest and enthusiasm (Green and Hooper 239-240). That may well be, but Lewis seems to have already had the story in his mind, and he already had the example of his friends Owen Barfield and J.R.R. Tolkien writing children's stories.

If one can actually "explain" creative outbursts such as the one which produced the Narnia Chronicles, it might also be well to remember that in 1948 Lewis's adoptive mother, Mrs. Janie Moore, was placed permanently in a nursing home, where she eventually died in

1951. While this circumstance may have carried Lewis back emotionally to his own childhood and the loss of his birth mother, it also seems to have freed him from a rather onerous share of domestic duties (Green and Hooper 229-230).

Whatever served as the catalyst for the actual composition of the Narnia stories, it remains intriguing that Lewis, then in his sixties, should recall having the image in his mind of a faun with an umbrella since he was "about sixteen." At about that age—seventeen, to be precise—Lewis had a truly life-changing literary experience, his discovery of George MacDonald's *Phantastes*. When he first read the story in the spring of 1916, Lewis wrote enthusiastically to his childhood friend Arthur Greeves that he'd had a "great literary experience" that week (*Stand* 94) and the book became a lifelong favourite of his. In his preface to the MacDonald anthology which he edited, Lewis wrote that he "crossed a great frontier" when he first read *Phantastes* (MacDonald 25) and that the book baptized his imagination, giving him a sense of the "divine, magical, terrifying, and ecstatic reality in which we all live" (MacDonald 26-27).

As a child himself, Lewis had been no great reader of children's stories, with the exception of Edith Nesbit's tales of adventurous neighbourhood boys and girls (Green and Hooper 236). So it was not perhaps until his reading of *Phantastes* that Lewis first felt the emotional depth and spiritual richness that a fantasy story could contain. As mentioned above, Lewis himself recognized the influence of Edith Nesbit on the Chronicles. But one wonders also about the influence of MacDonald.

That Faun with an umbrella which Lewis had carried in his imagination for over thirty years became, of course, Mr. Tumnus in *The Lion, the Witch and the Wardrobe*, who invites Lucy to his cozy little cave, where he lights a lamp, offers her a spot of tea, originally planning to lull her to sleep and then betray her to the White Witch.

Though Tumnus is too decent a Faun to go through with the scheme, his behaviour, and the terrible woman he fears, call to mind the Maid of the Alders in *Phantastes*. She too is a white lady who is both beautiful and cold; she too invites the protagonist, Anodos, to her cave, where she lights a lamp and lulls him to sleep. And she too plans to betray Anodos to the evil Ash-Tree, though, unlike Tumnus, she has no second thoughts about her scheme: Anodos escapes with his life only through the good offices of a passing knight (51-54).

After that early episode in *The Lion, the Witch and the Wardrobe*, the rest of the book reminds us rather more of Edith Nesbit, though with sprightlier prose and with rich spiritual overtones, and rather less of George MacDonald. When he had finished the first book, however, Lewis originally intended to tell the story of Narnia's origins, featuring Professor Kirke as a boy named Digory, along with his friend Polly. This book, which eventually became *The Magician's Nephew*, was, as mentioned above, Lewis's greatest creative challenge in the series and the only one in which he composed significant fragments of narrative which were never used.

Lewis's original beginning, which he eventually set aside, is now called "The Lefay Fragment" and is reprinted in Walter Hooper's *Past Watchful Dragons*, pages 48-65. This version begins on a strongly satirical note:

> Once there was a boy called Digory who lived with his Aunt because his father and mother were both dead. His Aunt, whose name was Gertrude, was not at all a nice person. Years ago she had been a schoolmistress and bullied the girls. Then she became the headmistress and bullied the mistresses. Then she became an inspector and bullied the headmistresses. Then she went into Parliament and became a Minister of something and bullied everybody. (*Dragons* 48)

After this acerbic opening, we soon learn that Digory was born with the gift of being able to communicate with trees and animals. As soon as his officious Aunt is out of the house, he goes out to the grove of trees behind his house and rests in the branch-arms of a friendly old Oak tree, while chatting with the Oak and a nearby Birch. Soon a squirrel named Pattertwig joins them, offering Digory a nut and complaining that humans don't seem to do much "except killing animals or putting them in cages or cutting down trees." Then he hastens to add, "No offence, Digory: we all know you're different" (52).

Soon Digory notices a girl in the backyard next door, trying to build something. Her name is Polly and, when she asks who Digory's been talking to, he keeps his gift a secret and says he's discovered a tame squirrel out in the woods. Polly wonders if they could catch it, and says she read in a book how to trap squirrels. Though she can only hear the chattering of a squirrel and the rustling of leaves, Digory hears Pattertwig taking offense at this conversation, while the Oak complains, "That's what comes of chattering with humans. I knew she'd been wanting to eat him or skin him or shut him up" (54-55).

Polly's building project is a raft, which she wants to launch in a nearby stream that flows into an underground culvert. She hopes to explore what she conceives to be "the bowels of the earth," planning to take along a torch and a pistol. Digory agrees to join the expedition, but notices that her raft needs another crosspiece to hold the logs together. Polly suggests that they saw a limb off the old Oak tree for that purpose. Digory hesitates at first, but Polly badgers him about not being able to use a saw, about being afraid of what the grown-ups might say, and about being a big baby, until finally he climbs up a wall and begins sawing off a branch. The Oak tree says nothing, but one of its limbs gives Digory a good swat in the face. As a thunderstorm descends, he insists on finishing the job before going inside to get out of the rain.

The next day Digory returns to the wood to apologize to the old Oak, but discovers to his horror that he can no longer talk to the trees or understand the language of animals and birds. He returns to his house feeling wretched and ashamed, where he meets his godmother, Mrs. Lefay, "the shortest and fattest woman he had ever seen" (63). She wears a black dress covered with gold dust, and carries a black bag holding her rabbit Coiny, out for his afternoon ride. Mrs. Lefay seems to know all about Digory's terrible secret, telling him he looks like Adam five minutes after he'd been driven out of the Garden of Eden. Seeming to have some sort of mission in mind for Digory, she gives him a card with her address on it, and offers complicated directions for finding a furniture shop which sells birds and pictures.

"Then you must go into the shop and you will see ..." The manuscript breaks off in the middle of Mrs. Lefay's instructions, literally halting in midsentence. What was it Digory was supposed to see? That was as far as Lewis got with his first opening of what would later become the "Genesis" of Narnia, *The Magician's Nephew*.

In the opening pages of *The Lion, the Witch and the Wardrobe*, there seemed to be an echo of *Phantastes* in the Tumnus episode. In this, what would have been the opening of the second Narnia book, the influence of MacDonald is even more apparent. When Anodos is led into the enchanted wood, he finds that he can speak to the trees and even understand the conversation of squirrels (*Phantastes* 40-42). He learns from a country maid that he can trust the Oak tree and should look after the delicate Birch (21). It seems that if Lewis began *The Lion, the Witch and the Wardrobe*, as he said, "in the tradition of E. Nesbit," he initially intended to continue the series more "in the tradition of G. MacDonald."

But, obviously he did not continue. One can only speculate as to why Lewis broke off this version of the story, though the reasons may not be all that obscure. On hearing this narrative, Roger Lancelyn Green complained that Mrs. Lefay seemed too much like a burlesque of a fairy godmother and apparently Lewis was inclined to agree (*Dragons* 66).

Also, Lefay, in her own quirky way, seems to be a practitioner of "good magic." By this time in his life, Lewis seems to have concluded that there was no such thing. As he explained in *The Abolition of Man*, magic like science was an attempt to deny one's finitude, one's creatureliness:

> There is something which unites magic and applied science while separating both from the "wisdom" of earlier ages. For the wise men of old the cardinal problem had been how to conform the soul to reality, and the solution had been knowledge, self-discipline, and virtue. For magic and applied science alike the problem is how to subdue reality to the wishes of men. (87-88)

Many students of the occult distinguish between white magic, used only for constructive purposes such as healing or enhancing fertility, and black magic, the casting of spells and curses. Lewis, of course, was aware of the distinction, but he doubted whether it were as clear-cut as sometimes maintained. In his volume of the *Oxford History of English*

Literature, he explains the difference between *magia*, high or "white" magic, such as we encounter in Merlin or Bercilek, which is associated with the world of Faerie, and *goeteia*, black magic, associated with witchcraft and Faustian contracts with the devil. But having made the distinction, Lewis adds that most sixteenth-century writers, including King James himself (who published his *Demonology* in 1597) condemned all kinds of magic as a snare, warning that even "white magic" was a danger to the soul (7-8). He illustrated this point in *That Hideous Strength: A Modern Fairy-Tale for Grown-Ups*, where even the faithful Merlin is told by Ransom that he has been awakened from an enchanted slumber partly so that his own soul might be saved (289) and that even his practice of "good magic" has withered his spirit (285).

By the time Mrs. Lefay is mentioned in *The Magician's Nephew*, Lewis seemed to have gotten this issue straight in his mind. There she is alluded to as a *bad* fairy godmother, creating the magic rings which can so easily be put to evil purposes and ending up in prison (16-19).

Apart from the ambiguity about Mrs. Lefay's moral nature, Lewis seemed to break some of his own story-telling "rules" in this first attempt. In the preface to *That Hideous Strength*, Lewis explains that fantasy stories should be anchored in the "real world"; their characters begin in ordinary circumstances until they are swept into the world of Faerie (7). But in this version Digory is *born* enchanted, able to speak to trees and animals with no explanation given.

Lewis also warned about not letting the "expository demon" take over in a children's story. In "Sometimes Fairy Stories May Say Best What's to be Said," he explains that a creative writer has to find the proper balance between the Artist, who wants to tell a good story, and the Man, who wants to share his convictions and worldview in his narrative (*Worlds* 35-37). In the Lefay fragment, we see too much of Lewis the Man. Before the story has fairly gotten started, we have some rather heavy-handed satire on contemporary education and a few too many references to humans abusing the environment. That is certainly a worthy issue, but in this draft that oft-repeated theme seems to stifle the plot.

For whatever reason, Lewis abandoned this fragment altogether and later started afresh. Of course, that is not to say the creative effort here was wasted. As we already know, Digory and Polly would reappear in *The Magician's Nephew*, where's Digory's Adamic "Fall" would be less ecological and more theological. Pattertwig makes his appearance as one of the Talking Animals in *Prince Caspian*, and Aunt Gertrude turns up as the Head of Experiment House in *The Silver Chair*. (In that version, she gets her comeuppance—being elected to Parliament—not at the beginning of the story, but at the end.)

Lewis seems to have gone down one more creative cul de sac in his composition of *The Magician's Nephew*, a passage where Digory stayed at an old farmhouse in Charn with a cottager named Piers and his wife, who are eventually dragged into Narnia, where they become its first king and queen. Roger Lancelyn Green, on reading this section, found their northern "Loamshire" dialect too difficult and their speeches long-winded, causing the story to drag. Lewis struck upon the happy idea of deleting these characters and supplying the simple, honest Frank, the hackney coachman, and his wife to be the first royal couple of Narnia (Green and Hooper 247-48).

The "Piers fragment" has not survived, which some might argue is appropriate, since Lewis never intended it for publication. To others like myself, though, it seems a pity. As the Lefay fragment shows, for someone of extraordinary creative powers like Lewis, even artistic "failures" can be more intriguing than the "successes" of many a writer with lesser gifts.

DAVID C. DOWNING

David C. Downing is the R.W. Schlosser Professor of English at Elizabethtown College in Lancaster County, Pennsylvania. Downing did his undergraduate work at Westmont College in California and the University of

Colorado. He earned his doctorate in English from the University of California, Los Angeles.

Downing's first book on C.S. Lewis is *Planets in Peril: A Critical Study of C.S. Lewis's Ransom Trilogy* (University of Massachusetts Press, 1992). *Planets in Peril* was honoured as the Mythopoeic Society's Book of the Year. Downing's second Lewis book is *The Most Reluctant Convert: C.S. Lewis's Journey to Faith* (InterVarsity, 2002). This was named by the American Library Association as one of the Top Ten Books of the Year in the category of Religion. The book was released as an audiobook in December 2003 and has been translated into Italian, Portuguese, and Korean.

In 2005 Downing published two new books on C.S. Lewis, *Into the Region of Awe: Mysticism in C.S. Lewis* (InterVarsity) and *Into the Wardrobe: C.S. Lewis and the Narnia Chronicles* (Jossey-Bass). In addition to his books, Downing has been a contributor to or consulting editor for *The Canadian C.S. Lewis Journal, Christianity Today, Christianity and Literature, Books and Culture, Christian Scholar's Review, Seven*, and *The Bulletin of the New York C.S. Lewis Society*. His forthcoming book is a departure from Lewis studies: it is *A South Divided: Portraits of Dissent in the Confederacy*.

WORKS CITED

- Carpenter, Humphrey. *The Inklings*. London: George Allen and Unwin, 1978.

- Green, Roger Lancelyn and Walter Hooper. *C.S. Lewis: A Biography*. New York: Harcourt Brace Jovanovich, 1974.

- Hooper, Walter. *Past Watchful Dragons: The Narnian Chronicles of C.S. Lewis*. New York: Collier, 1979.

- Lewis, C.S. *The Abolition of Man*. New York: Macmillan, 1973. Orig. pub. 1943.

- ————. *English Literature in the Sixteenth Century, Excluding Drama*. Oxford: Clarendon Press, 1954.

- —————. *George Macdonald: An Anthology Edited by C.S. Lewis*. New York: Macmillan, 1947.

- —————. *The Magician's Nephew*. New York: Collier, 1955. Rpt. 1970.

- —————. *Of Other Worlds: Essays and Stories*. Ed. by Walter Hooper. New York: Harcourt Brace Jovanovich, 1966.

- —————. *That Hideous Strength: A Modern Fairy Tale for Grown-Ups*. New York: Macmillan, 1968. Orig. pub. London: John Lane, Bodley Head, 1945; New York: Macmillan, 1946.

- —————. *They Stand Together: The Letters of C.S. Lewis to Arthur Greeves (1914-1963)*. Ed. by Walter Hooper. London: Collins, 1979.

- MacDonald, George. *Phantastes and Lilith*. Grand Rapids, Michigan: William B. Eerdmans Publishing Co., 1964.

- Walker, Andrew and James Patrick, eds. *A Christian for All Christians: Essays in Honour of C.S. Lewis*. Washington, D.C.: Regnery Gateway, 1992.

- Wilson, A.N. *C.S. Lewis: A Biography*. New York: W. W. Norton and Company, 1990.

TO NARNIA AND BACK

By Martha A. Emmert

For years I longed for just such an adventure. Now it had come. What could be better than a return to the world of C.S. Lewis where the magic of Narnia began? I could still remember standing with Stephen Schofield, the founding editor of *The Canadian C.S. Lewis Journal*, in 1985, as he showed me a path through a lovely English wood. It stood quietly drowsing under the luminous green of afternoon sunlight shining through its leafy cover. "This is a walk that Lewis often took," he said. We looked at one another a minute, then exclaimed together, "The Wood between the Worlds!"

The very map of England is alight with names and places I have heard since earliest years ... Banberry, Drury Lane, Sherwood Forest, Nottingham, London Bridge. This, too, helped make the visit seem like a return to the joys of childhood.

And so my husband, Leon, and I joined the Wheaton Alumni Academic Tour, June 3-14, 1995, to the Oxford of C.S. Lewis and the London of Dorothy L. Sayers. Our respect for and debt to Lewis seemed a reasonable basis for our acceptance of one another, though we met as strangers to begin with.

Our group soon formed a fellowship. For those of us who have read Lewis diligently and often, it was not so much new material that we sought but the illumination of sights and sounds familiar to him which might shed light on words meaning so much to us. As on a quest, we journeyed together. Did we unconsciously yearn for a portion of his spirit to fall on us?

The tour proved magnificent information from our English guide, Rosalind Hutchinson, from our study guide, Marjorie Lamp Mead, and from the various others prepared to speak to us. We were served until our cups ran over from such individuals as Barbara Reynolds, George Sayer, Douglas Gresham and Christopher Dean.

We stayed at the Eastgate Hotel in Oxford where Lewis met Helen Joy Davidman Gresham for tea. It is very near to Magdalen College where his rooms were. While still awaiting our room key I had the joy of seeing and recognizing Peter Cousin, the legendary cab driver and member of the Oxford C.S. Lewis Society, talking to Marjorie Mead. I wish I had met him.

Among our first forays into Oxford we experienced the wonderful University Church of St. Mary the Virgin where Lewis preached "The Weight of Glory" in June 1941.

It seemed like a dream to actually see the Eagle and Child and to enter in and take refreshments. How intimate the photo-haunted room where those faces once sat and drank and read, challenging one another or roaring in mutual mirth! The good fellowship they shared still shone from the aging photos. I felt a pang of loss such as one feels contemplating the end of the round table, its circle of Knights and its good King Arthur.

Meeting George Sayer was a high point. We drove to "Hameworth" in Malvern, the hospitable home visited by C.S. Lewis, J.R.R Tolkien and others. George had much to share.

George Sayer accompanied us to Malvern Priory and Malvern College, where both Lewis brothers—Clive and Warren—attended and George later taught English. A moment of meaning came to me when George pointed out the dorm windows of the schoolboy C.S. Lewis. We were standing just above the broad green playing fields of the school. I thought of the bane sports proved to be in Lewis's school years and recalled anew his wish to be safe in the library we had just visited.

I felt privileged to meet Douglas Gresham, the youngest stepson of C.S. Lewis. Douglas met us at the Oxford Crematorium, "Garden of Remembrance," where Joy, his mother, was cremated and where Lewis placed a stone plaque to her memory. It is truly a garden where 23,000 roses flourish.

Douglas is a very intense person and a committed Christian. With his seriousness and compassion I could see why he was such a comfort to his stepfather in their shared loss. He holds crisp and clear-cut beliefs and speaks with a passion and forthrightness he may well have learned from his mother. Douglas led us to Headington Quarry's Holy Trinity Church where we visited the common grave of both Clive and Warren Lewis. The inscriptions are nearly impossible to read due to discoloration of the cement cover. The grave in no way indicates to the world the monumental impact C.S. Lewis's witness has had on so many lives in so many diverse places.

Inside the parish church itself, I remembered how he practiced assembling with other Christians for worship and communion. I could visualize him in his corner by the pillar towards the back.

Charles Kimber, sexton for many years, was on hand to reminisce. He showed an 850-year-old chalice which Lewis used for communion. Kimber attended the funerals of both Lewis brothers. Recently the Memorial Etched Window of Narnia motifs has been installed nearest to where C.S. Lewis habitually sat. (I like the window, but I looked in vain for Puddleglum!)

We followed Douglas through the Kilns, C.S. Lewis's home from 1930-63. Douglas lived there from 1956-63, between ages of ten and seventeen. When Lewis died, Douglas went to his guardian, Jean Wakeman, a close friend of his mother. Jean lives near Studley Priory where we ate that evening as a group and Douglas addressed us late into the night.

Dr. J. Stanley Mattson's C.S. Lewis Foundation wants to restore the Kilns as a Study Centre but lacks funds. It is now rented to Oxford students to help pay expenses and upkeep. Major repairs have already been done and the roof replaced.

Douglas pointed out the downstairs bedroom where C.S. Lewis died and showed the office and sitting room built on for Warnie. I am sorry the estate could not have been preserved as it was when purchased by the Lewis brothers with such delight. There is a home now between the Kilns and the pond and one can see dwellings in nearly every direction, not at all the vision which imagination and reading have maintained in my mind.

Addison's Walk seemed very familiar and precious and I felt the closest perhaps to the spirit of C.S. Lewis as I toured his college and walked this walk, so meaningful in his spiritual birth and life.

Spiritually, I am not as indebted to Dorothy L. Sayers. I have long read her Lord Peter Wimsey stories for pleasure and am only recently collecting her *The Mind of the Maker*, *The Man Born to be King: A Play-Cycle on the Life of our Lord and Saviour Jesus Christ* and other writings. I admire her intellect and wit and the ability to state her convictions clearly.

In Oxford we photographed her birth place (marked with a plaque) and toured Somerville College where she took her degree. I even stood at the High Table where she gave her speech on "The Value of an Oxford Education."

We spent a day at Canterbury, touring the old city and Cathedral. We saw the Hall where Dorothy's play, *The Zeal of Thy House*, was performed.

We met Christopher Dean, Chairman of the Dorothy L. Sayers Society. He led us on a walking tour of Bloomsbury, a part of London Dorothy knew well and used in her detective books.

On our final evening together we feasted at Rules Restaurant, the oldest one in London. Dorothy Sayers often dined there with other detective writers. (It was where she has Lord Peter Wimsey proposing to Harriet Vane.)

We had wonderful food and a fine festive spirit. The cooks paraded, roast held high, before carving to enthusiastic applause. A birthday cake for Barbara Reynolds capped the meal.

Barbara, a friend of Sayers and her biographer, spoke after the meal. When she taught at Wheaton College, Wheaton, Illinois, she founded the journal, *SEVEN: An Anglo-American Literary Review*, which is still being published, celebrating seven authors associated with C.S. Lewis and Dorothy L. Sayers.

And now I am back home to the daily and familiar, but the magic of this trip to Narnia and back will live long in my heart.

MARTHA ATKINS EMMERT

Martha Atkins Emmert was born in Iowa in 1923 and educated through High School. She became a Christian on January 14, 1942, and began to prepare for ministry in foreign missions. She graduated in 1949 from Northern Baptist Theological Seminary in Chicago and continued in preparation.

She married Rev. Leon Emmert of Topeka, Indiana, in 1948. They studied one year in Brussels, Belgium, before service in the then Belgian Congo. They served there with American Baptist International Ministries until retirement in 1990.

The Emmerts have two children, Daniel Emmert of Fort Wayne, Indiana, and Michal Rose Emmert-Hart, an Art Therapist working in Staunton, Virginia.

Martha published her memoirs in 1997, *Common Clay*.

The Lion, the Witch and the Wardrobe: Through Eight-Year-Old Eyes

Collected by Roger J. Stronstad

Editor's note: Roger Stronstad collected the following thoughts on **The Lion, the Witch and the Wardrobe** *from several eight-year-olds in a Grade 2 class of students in an Abbotsford, British Columbia, school. They were chosen on the nebulous basis of their "interest" to an adult reader. Both the teacher and the students are anonymous. He writes: "I grew up in a family of readers and have read copiously from early childhood. I first read Lewis during my student days at university, but I did not read the Chronicles of Narnia until I was thirty-one years old. Thus, I missed the sheer delight that* **The Lion, the Witch and the Wardrobe** *... evokes in the young readers for whom the story was written. ... Eight-year-old readers share with us their impressions and insights upon reading* **The Lion, the Witch and the Wardrobe** *for the first time." We have elected to retain their individual style, misspellings and all!*

1. I think C.S. Lewis is a very talented writer. I like a lot of his books. But I'm only going to tell you about one. It's my favourite one, too, *The Lion, the Witch and the Wardrobe*. I like Peter most like how he's high king of Narnia. Also how he is a young knight. Speaking of knights, in the end Edmund becomes a knight. It's pretty sneaky of Susan and Lucy to get up in the middle of the night and follow Aslan without anybody noticing them.

2. I thought the book about *The Lion, the Witch and the Wardrobe* was fascinating because it had lots of action. I liked the part when Peter, Susan, Edmund and Lucy rode on Aslan's back to the Witch's castle to free all the statues in there. The part I didn't like was when they fought and fought and fought. The funny part was when Aslan roared and scared all the enemies away.

3. I think the most boringest part was when the White Witch threw Asland onto the stone tabble and killed him. It was not scary at all, not even one bit. And then the part where Mr. Temnus was turned into stone—now that was interesting very much. Then when there was the part where the White Witch gave Edmund turckish-dealight that was a little good but it was boring still. The part that I liked the most was wear Lucy said to Mr. Tumnus, "O MR. TUMNUS, DO STOP IT AT WONES." Now that was funny, yup, that was!! And the part where Lucy walked into the wardrowb, that was OK, I guess.

4. This is what I think about *The Lion, the Witch and the Wardrobe*. I think that the book is really good because I liked it when Lucy went into the wardrobe and came into Narnia and met Mr. Tumnus and then Mr. Tumnus took Lucy to his house. I also liked the part when Mr. Tunnus started to cry. I also thought the White Witch was weird and her dwarf. It was sad when the White Witch tied up Aslan. It was scary when Aslan came back to life. I have almost all the C.S. Lewis books.

5. I think C.S. Lewis is a great author. I don't like the part when the white witch kills Asland. I think it was evil when Mr. Tumnus was going to hand Lucy over to the White Witch. I think Edmund was bad to try to be prince of Narnia with the White Witch. I think Asland was nice to give up his life for Edmund to live.

6. These are my opinions about *The Lion, the Witch and the Wardrobe* by C.S. Lewis. My favourite character is Lucy because she is sweet, very kind, and she has a very good imagination. I think it was sad when the White Witch killed Aslan. But the good thing is he came back to life. It was really neat when Edmund changed the way he acted in the middle of the story. The story had a lot of detailed words.

7. C.S. Lewis books are cool! I like Lucy because I think she's cute and funny. I also think it would be cool to have a wand like the White Witch. I would turn my anyoing little sister to stone. I almost cried when the White Witch tied up Aslan and killed him on the stone table. But my tears went away when he came back to life and freed the other animals from being stone! And I've always wondered when reading *The Lion, the Witch and the Wardrobe*, whatever did happen to the White Witch? And that's why I think C.S. Lewis books are cool!

8. I'm going to tell you about *The Lion, the Witch and the Wardrobe*. My opinion about it is that I hate all of the bad guys. Because they are all nasty. The stuff I like is when the four kids, Lucy, Edmund, Susan, and finally Peter. It sounds cool when the stone table cracks in half. The part that is boring is the part when the kids at the start are playing hide-and-go-seek. That story is … REMARKABLE! It was soo dreadful when Aslan was tied up! C.S. Lewis is so, so experimental with his stories. He is so imaginative with his stories.

THE LION, THE WITCH AND THE WARDROBE AT 50: A CELEBRATION (AND A WORRY)

By Paul F. Ford

... It is the author who *intends*; the book *means*. The author's intention is that which, if it is realized, will in his eyes constitute success...the meaning of a book is the series or systems of emotions, reflections, and attitudes produced by reading it...this product differs with different readers.... The ideally true or right meaning would be that shared...by the largest number of the best readers after repeated and careful readings over several generations, different periods, nationalities, moods, degrees of alertness, private preoccupations, states of health, spirits, and the like cancelling one another out when...they cannot be fused so as to enrich one another.[1]

That the readers of *The Lion, the Witch and the Wardrobe* now number in the millions and that their ranks will grow in this new millennium are incontestable. I suspect that one of the joys of heaven will be able to sit in the company of C.S. Lewis and all the readers (and re-readers!) of *The Lion, the Witch and the Wardrobe* to share the meaning of this marvelous book and how it enriched each of us. The very sharing would be a mystagogy, a farther up and farther in increase of grace,

grace given by the not safe but good One by his death, resurrection, rescue of those turned to stone, killing of His killer, crowning of regents, and quiet slipping away to return again. What a grace! Such a sharing! This essay, far from being the appreciation[2] *The Lion, the Witch and the Wardrobe* deserves, is better read as an invitation to this celestial celebration.

Before I began writing this essay, it had been at least three years since I re-read *The Lion, the Witch and the Wardrobe* for my contributions to *The C.S. Lewis Readers' Encyclopedia*.[3] I first read *The Lion, the Witch and the Wardrobe* thirty-three years ago when I was recovering from the flu as a junior (third-year student) in a seminary (boarding) college. For the five years previous I had been reading all of Lewis I could get my hands on. I never knew he had written children's books until I discovered them in a bookshop. Buying them rather shamefacedly (like Susan Pevensie, I wanted to appear "beyond" such childish things), I did not display them on my seminary bookshelves. However, there came the time when, sick of and in my new school, I took them out one by one and read them furtively, quickly hiding each under my bed covers whenever a fellow seminarian visited me.

I will never forget my joy when, in chapter fifteen, "Deeper Magic from Before the Dawn of Time," Aslan invites Susan and Lucy to romp with him. For the first time I felt the elation of Christ's rising to new life. Of course there were other delights: the home-iness of Mr. Tumnus's cave and the Beavers' Lodge, the thrill of the first pronunciation of Aslan's name (the pivotal thirty-fifth and thirty-sixth full paragraphs of chapter seven, "A Day with the Beavers," more about this shortly), the end of winter and the return of spring, and terrors, and revulsion (at Edmund's betrayal of Lucy). But Lewis succeeded in his goal of helping me get past the watchful dragons at the Sunday school door[4] so that I could, almost for the first time, have my own feelings about Christian realities.

Since that first reading, I have re-read *The Lion, the Witch and the Wardrobe* at least twenty times. I *analyzed* the book and its sisters almost a dozen times for *Companion to Narnia* (I hope its readers do not think I *dissected* the books), but my best re-readings have happened when my spirits were low. Then the books served as a seven-volume magician's book which disenchanted all that should be disenchanted and re-enchanted all that should be enchanted. Here I am deliberately evoking Lucy's use of Coriakin's Book in *The Voyage of the "Dawn Treader"* and Lewis's magnificent sermon, "The Weight of Glory":

> "Remember your fairy tales. Spells are used for breaking enchantments as well as for inducing them. And you and I have need of the strongest spell that can be found to wake us from the evil enchantment of worldliness which has been laid upon us for nearly a hundred years."[5]

As I have said, I had not read *The Lion, the Witch and the Wardrobe* for at least three years. I had tried twice and failed to read *The Magician's Nephew* as the first of the Chronicles, as the marketers of the "new" editions[6] would wish (the "worry" of the title of this essay, and I will come to it soon). Asked to write for *The Canadian C.S. Lewis Journal* (may God reward the late Stephen Schofield and his wife, and the editors who kept Stephen's dream alive!), I took up the "new" hardcover edition of *The Lion, the Witch and the Wardrobe* and tried to imagine what a reader might have experienced when s/he read the first edition that autumn of 1950 (sometime after October 16 in the British Commonwealth and after November 7 in the United States of America[7]). The key to reading the Chronicles is, I reminded myself, "reading with the heart," in the apt phrase of Peter Schakel.[8]

The most important fact I had to *forget* in this re-reading is that *The Lion, the Witch and the Wardrobe* is the first of what later grew to be seven Chronicles of Narnia, a name they received from Roger Lancelyn Green only in 1952.[9] In fact, when Lewis finished the book, in the spring of 1949, there were no others planned. (He soon began to write what later became *The Magician's Nephew*, which ended up being the last Chronicle he completed.)[10] I also had to forget that it had taken Lewis nearly ten years to return to and finish *The Lion, the Witch and the Wardrobe*, a book he began at the outset of World War II when girls from London were evacuated to his home outside of Oxford. (I am happy to reproduce in the appendix to this essay the text of a letter I received from one of these girls.)

What came across strongly to me on this re-reading was how the narrative tastes of the children's books of Edith Nesbit.[11] We know that Lewis loved her Bastable books (and even refers to the Bastable family in the second paragraph of chapter one of *The Magician's Nephew*) and how some motifs from her stories *The Magic City* (1911) and "The Aunt and Amabel" (in *The Magic World*, 1912) went down very deep in Lewis's imagination, only to come up in *The Lion, the Witch and the Wardrobe*.[12] The omniscient author's perspective, with a touch of the avuncular (all the talk about not shutting the wardrobe door) is alive in Nesbit and in Lewis. Lewis was saying a great deal when he told Chad Walsh in the summer of 1948 that he was "completing a children's book he has begun 'in the tradition of E. Nesbit'" when he had finished *Surprised by Joy: The Shape of My Early Life* (*C.S. Lewis: Apostle to the Skeptics* [1949], p. 10).[13]

It is very significant that Lewis was writing his autobiography about the paralysis of his spiritual life caused by the death of his mother and the Great Magician's [God's] failure to answer prayer, at the same time he was writing *The Lion, the Witch and the Wardrobe*, whose central motif is the rescue of a country and a boy from the paralysis of winter and betrayal, respectively. It appears that one of the reasons that Lewis delayed finishing his autobiography is that he was swept up in the creation of the Narnian stories. These stories allowed him to deal at the feeling level with the death of his mother (in *The Magician's Nephew*) and the estrangement from his father (glimpsed in Tirian's meeting with his father Erlian in chapter sixteen of *The Last Battle*[14]) and, most importantly, with the ever good but never tame Lion of Narnia. The at least fictional resolution of Lewis's central spiritual crisis is framed by two scenes in *The Magician's Nephew*, the scene at the beginning of chapter twelve, "Strawberry's Adventure," and the scene at the end of chapter fourteen, "The Planting of the Tree":

> "Yes," said Digory. He had had for a second some wild idea of saying "I'll try to help you if you'll promise to help my Mother," but he realized in time that the Lion was not at all the sort of person one could try to make bargains with. But when he had said "Yes," he thought of his Mother, and he thought of the great hopes he had had, and how they were all

dying away, and a lump came in his throat and tears in his eyes, and he blurted out: "But please, please, won't you, can't you give me something that will cure Mother?" Up till then he had been looking at the Lion's great feet and the huge claws on them; now, in his despair, he looked up at its face. What he saw surprised him as much as anything in his whole life. For the tawny face was bent down near his own and (wonder of wonders) great shining tears stood in the Lion's eyes. They were such big, bright tears compared with Digory's own that for a moment he felt as if the Lion must really be sorrier about his Mother than he was himself. "My son, my son," said Aslan. "I know. Grief is great. Only you and I in this land know that yet. Let us be good to one another..."

"... and the Witch tempted you to do another thing, my son, did she not?" "Yes, Aslan. She wanted me to take an apple home to Mother." "Understand, then, that it would have healed her; but not to your joy or hers. The day would have come when both you and she would have looked back and said it would have been better to die in that illness." And Digory could say nothing, for tears choked him and he gave up all hopes of saving his Mother's life; but at the same time he knew that the Lion knew what would have happened, and that there might be things more terrible even than losing someone you love by death. But now Aslan was speaking again, almost in a whisper: "That is what would have happened, child, with a stolen apple. It is not what will happen now. What I give you now will bring joy. It will not, in your world, give endless life, but it will heal. Go. Pluck her an apple from the Tree."

Such enormous, indeed tragic, feelings were only hinted at in *The Lion, the Witch and the Wardrobe*. But all four children, especially Edmund, are quite disoriented by being evacuated from wartime London and separated from their parents. In addition Edmund has been influenced for the worst by a "horrid school which was where he had begun to go wrong."[15] (Alas, the strong, negative hint given by the kind of animal Edmund hopes to see while at the Professor's estate, "snakes"—introduced into all the American editions by Lewis himself—has been suppressed in favour of "foxes" in all British editions.[16]) However, far from hints, what are clear and unmistakable on every page, beginning with the advent of Father Christmas[17] in chapter ten, "The Spell Begins to Break," are the effects of Aslan's return, in first the sounds, then the sights, and finally the smells of spring come to Narnia. Thus cavalcade ends the beholding of Aslan for the very first time, one of the most significant passages in the book.

> But as for Aslan himself, the Beavers and the children didn't know what to do or say when they saw him. People who have not been in Narnia sometimes think that a thing cannot be good and terrible at the same time. If the children had ever thought so, they were cured of it now. For when they tried to look at Aslan's face they just caught a glimpse of the golden mane and the great, royal, solemn, overwhelming eyes; and then they found they couldn't look at him and went all trembly.[18]

This experience of the simultaneous terror and delight, the *mysterium tremendum et fascinans* of Rudolf Otto's *The Idea of the Holy*, one of Lewis's ten favorite books,[19] has been anticipated in the thirty-fifth and thirty-sixth full paragraphs of chapter seven, "A Day with the Beavers." Mr. Beaver says, after much caution at being overheard, "They say Aslan is on the move—perhaps has already landed."

> And now a very curious thing happened. None of the children knew who Aslan was any more than you do; but the moment the Beaver had spoken these words everyone felt quite different. Perhaps it has sometimes happened to you in a dream that someone says something which you don't understand but in the dream it feels as if it had some enormous meaning, either a terrifying one which turns the whole dream into a nightmare or else a lovely meaning too lovely to put into words, which makes the dream so beautiful that you remember it all your life and are always wishing you could get into that dream again. It was like that now.[20] At the name of Aslan each one of the children felt something jump in its inside. Edmund felt a sensation of mysterious horror. Peter felt suddenly brave and

adventurous. Susan felt as if some delicious smell or some delightful strain of music had just floated by her. And Lucy got the feeling you have when you wake up in the morning and realize that it is the beginning of the holidays or the beginning of summer.

What is also obvious and splendid but so much more solemn is Edmund's reconciliation with the good and terrible Aslan and with his brother and sisters. No wonder that such an experience should have made him a graceful and quiet man, great in council, King Edmund the Just.[21]

After my most recent re-reading I also felt how complete in itself the story was and how satisfying, if read with the heart. The book seems to come to an end in the twenty-second full paragraph of chapter sixteen, "The Hunting of the White Stag": "So they lived in great joy and if ever they remembered their life in this world it was only as one remembers a dream." I grew convinced that C.S. Lewis added the last two sentences in the book only when he decided to write more books in the year after he finished *The Lion, the Witch and the Wardrobe*. "And that is the very end of the adventure of the wardrobe. But if the Professor was right it was only the beginning of the adventures of Narnia."

Here is where I must express my worry. Beginning with the worldwide editions published in 1994 the decision was made to market the Chronicles in the order of their internal chronology rather than in the order in which they were published from 1950-94 (what Doris Myers calls the chronological order as opposed to the canonical order). The HarperCollins web site now announces:

> The seven books of *The Chronicles of Narnia* were published between 1950 and 1956. *The Lion, the Witch and the Wardrobe* came first. It was because of the popularity of this book that the other books were written. But the author later expressed a wish that the books be sequenced by Narnian chronology, rather than the order in which they were first published. Thus the series now begins with *The Magician's Nephew*, in which the world of Narnia is created, and ends

with *The Last Battle*, in which it is destroyed, so that a new world can begin.[22]

My worry is that this decision will diminish their impact on future readers, indeed will impede readers from moving from *The Magician's Nephew* to *The Lion, the Witch and the Wardrobe* and thus to the end. Consider how *The Lion, the Witch and the Wardrobe* introduces the mystery of a world within a wardrobe and builds to the revelation of Aslan. Contrariwise, *The Magician's Nephew* plops the reader unmysteriously into the plot of the whole series, using "Narnia" as the fortieth word a reader will now encounter.

But the pivotal insight which clinches the argument for reading *The Lion, the Witch, and the Wardrobe* first is found in the scene cited above: "None of the children knew who Aslan was *any more than you do*; but the moment the Beaver had spoken these words everyone felt quite different." The five words I have emphasized show that we must read the books in the order in which they first came to the attention of the world of readers and re-readers, in the order in which the *meaning* of these glorious books grew beyond Lewis's late-formed *intention* to revise them. Here I am referring to a sentence in the epigraph of this essay: "It is the author who *intends*; the book *means*." C.S. Lewis's intention to emend the books, agreed to just two days before he died, is inferior to his attention to their meaning and their success at that level (his deeper intention). This deeper intention (I am tempted to call it the "Deeper Magic") was never better expressed than in Lewis's letter to Anne of March 5, 1961 (referring, it would seem, to her question about the twelfth-from-the-last paragraph of chapter sixteen of *The Silver Chair*):

> What Aslan meant when he said that he had died is, in one sense, plain enough. Read the earlier book in this series called The *Lion, the Witch and the Wardrobe*, and you will find the full story of how he was killed by the White Witch and came to life again. When you have read that, I think you will probably see that there is a deeper meaning behind it. The whole Narnian story is about Christ. That is to say, I asked myself, 'Supposing that there really was a world like Narnia and supposing it had (like our world) gone wrong and supposing

Christ wanted to go into that world and save it (as He did ours) what might have happened?' The stories are my answers. Since Narnia is a world of Talking Beasts, I thought He would become a Talking Beast there, as He became a man here. I pictured him becoming a lion there because (a) the lion is supposed to be the kings of beasts; (b) Christ is called 'the Lion of Judah' in the Bible; (c) I'd been having strange dreams about lions when I began writing the work. The whole series works out like this.

The Magician's Nephew tells the Creation and how evil entered Narnia.

The Lion etc the Crucifixion and Resurrection.

Prince Caspian restoration of the true religion after corruption.

The Horse and His Boy the calling and conversion of the heathen.

The Voyage of the DAWN TREADER the spiritual life (especially in Reepicheep).

The Silver Chair the continuing war with the powers of darkness.

The Last Battle the coming of the Antichrist (the Ape). The end of the world and the Last Judgment.[24]

Here Lewis indicates that the redemption story is foundational to the meaning of the series. Even through the inconsistencies among the stories, I shudder to think what might have happened if Lewis had applied his waning energies to making the Narnian Chronicles more successful at a superficial level.

Most Lewis scholars I have read express the same worry. Doris Myers (in her essential essay, "Growing in Grace: The Anglican Spiritual Style in the Narnia Chronicles"[25]), Colin N. Manlove,[26] Peter Schakel,[27] and now Emma Dunbar[28] all argue to retain the original order of publication. Schakel says it most succinctly:

The only reason to read *The Magician's Nephew* first ... is for the chronological order of events, and that, as every storyteller knows, is quite unimportant as a reason. Often the early events in a sequence have a greater impact or effect as a flashback, told after later events which provide background and establish perspective. So it is ... with the Chronicles. The artistry, the archetypes, and the pattern of Christian thought all make it preferable to read the books in the order of their publication.[29]

We will have to see how the new marketing strategy will work out. We can pray that if sales of the Chronicles diminish, a return to the canonical order will be ordered.

And, after all, the strategy is not consistent. Isn't it amazing that, whenever anything Narnian is marketed, it is *The Lion, the Witch and the Wardrobe* that is featured! Witness the Michael Hague wall calendars,[30] the seven special editions Walter Hooper mentions in his *C.S. Lewis: A Companion and Guide*,[31] a list which includes the glorious fully-illustrated Robin Laurie abridgement (how I wish he would finish the other six chronicles!), and the nine of the eleven projects since Hooper's book was published in 1996: 1) *Lucy Steps through the Wardrobe*, 2) *Edmund and the White Witch*, 3) *Aslan*, 4) *Aslan's Triumph*, 5) *The 1999 World of Narnia Calendar*, 6) *The Narnia Paper Dolls: The Lion, the Witch and the Wardrobe Collection* (these six books are illustrated by Deborah Maze), 7) *The Lion, the Witch and the Wardrobe: A 2001 Calendar*, 8) *The Lion, the Witch and the Wardrobe* (with illustrations by Christian Birmingham), and 9) *The Lion, the Witch and the Wardrobe* (pictures in black and white and full colour by Pauline Baynes). Only in 1999 did we see 10) *A Book of Narnians: The Lion, the Witch and the Others* (as well as a second edition of *The Land of Narnia: Brian Sibley Explores the World of C.S. Lewis*, originally published in 1989). And only in the year 2000 did we see an adapted and illustrated edition of a section of 11) *The Magician's Nephew: The Wood Between the Worlds*. But even the HarperCollins Classroom Activity Guide to the Chronicles of Narnia shows *The Lion, the Witch and the Wardrobe* as first on page two of the PDF file at their website.

So, Happy Birthday to *The Lion, the Witch and the Wardrobe*! May it find new readers for centuries to come so that readers will thrill at and know the name and the deeds of the Son of the Emperor-over-Seas.

EPILOGUE

[When I was a monk, with the name Bro. Peter Ford, I got in touch with one of the children billeted at the Kilns, Mrs. Margaret Leyland, and she supplied the other names, Mary Derrington and Katherine Fee (later killed in the Blitz with her parents). This letter was first published in *The Lamp-post of the Southern California C.S. Lewis Society* in July 1977.]

London, England

11 February 1977

Dear Brother Peter,

I was evacuated with my fellow students of the Convent of the Sacred Heart, Hammersmith, and was fortunate to be billeted (with two other girls) with Mrs. Moore at The Kilns, Headington, Oxford, from January-July 1940.

You may like to know something of the house; it was fairly large, stood in its own grounds which incorporated large lawns, flower beds, a tennis court, natural lake, copse and woodland leading up to Shotover, a large kitchen garden, a bungalow which we girls were allowed to use for our studies, and a summer house.

Mrs. Moore, a widow, lost her only son in the 1914-1918 war. C.S. Lewis and his brother, Major Lewis, were great friends of her son, and as their parents were dead Mrs. Moore adopted them, whether legally or not I do not know.

I saw little of Major Lewis as he was in the army, so the household consisted of Mrs. Moore, her daughter Kitty, C.S. Lewis, a cook, a parlour maid, and a gardener.

It was obvious that Mrs. Moore was devoted to Lewis; she was over-protective and I felt at the time she still thought him as a small boy; she called him 'Boyboys' and he called her 'Mintons.'

I shall always remember one warm, sunny spring day; we were all at lunch in the summer house, a distance of 20-30 yards from the house, when it grew overcast and before the meal was finished it started to rain quite heavily. Lunch over, Mrs. Moore rang for the parlour maid to ask her to fetch an umbrella and galoshes for Mr. Lewis so he could return to the house and not get wet. Lewis, I am certain, was liked and respected by his students. Often at weekends 3 or 4 came to the house (always male students; Mrs. Moore would, I am sure, not have taken kindly to females) and he played tennis with them and went swimming or boating on the lake. We girls joined in these activities; being school girls Mrs. Moore considered it safe for us to be with 'Boyboys.'

I was taking my School Certificate that June and Lewis was a great help to me, always interested and willing to give advice.

Mrs. Moore was very Victorian in her outlook and in her dress, and although I was 17 years old (the other 2 girls were younger) I was never allowed to have dinner with the family. We had supper which consisted every night of marie biscuits, an apple and a glass of milk. Without the help of Lewis and the cook we would have spent many a hungry night. The bedroom which we girls shared was above Lewis's study, which had a bay window with a flat roof. He used to pass food up to us and often helped us down so we could visit the kitchen where cook gave us food. Sometimes we climbed through the window of his study and listened to his records with him. On occasion he took us to the local fish and chip shop and we'd eat our secretive meal out of boxes on the way home.

One May morning he invited us to the top of Magdalen Tower to hear the singing. We often had tea with him after school in his rooms at college.

Once he took me to meet Masefield, and on another occasion I met Tolkien. It was then I heard Tolkien and Lewis discussing the 'Lord of the Rings' and I feel looking back that the embryo of the Narnia series began to take shape.

Lewis was a keen astronomer and had a telescope on the balcony of his bedroom. I was privileged to be shown many of the wonders of the universe.

He was a wonderful story teller and would tell us tales as we sat in the garden or walked through the woods and over Shotover.

He was unpretentious, a casual dresser preferring tweeds or grey flannels and sports jackets, usually carried a stout walking stick and always wore a deer-stalker hat.

He seemed unconcerned with the war, his mind being filled with space, the heavens, literature and his church. I think he was disappointed we girls were Catholics; he asked us once or twice to go and hear him preach (he was a lay preacher) and in return he came with us to Mass once or twice.

At that time I am certain he had no thought of becoming a Catholic and was not in favour of High Church Protestantism.

He was a kind, sympathetic and very human man, never talking down to us school girls. I shall always consider it a great privilege to have known him.

I hope these few details will be of assistance to you.

Yours sincerely,

Margaret M. Leyland (Mrs.)

PAUL F. FORD

Dr. Paul F. Ford has been reading C.S. Lewis since he was fifteen years old (since 1962) and has become an internationally recognized expert on the life and writings of C.S. Lewis and author of the award-winning book, *Companion to Narnia* (now in its fifth edition, HarperCollins, 2005) and of the *Pocket Companion to Narnia* (HarperCollins, 2005). His master's thesis was "The Life of the World to Come in the Writings of C.S. Lewis." His doctoral dissertation was "C.S. Lewis: Ecumenical Spiritual Director: A Study of His Experience and Theology of Prayer and Discernment in the Process of Becoming a Self." In 1974 he founded the Southern California C.S. Lewis Society. He serves as a board member of the Kilns Oxford Limited, a British charitable company that owns and (with the C.S. Lewis Foundation, Redlands, California) has restored Lewis's Oxford home. His most recent Lewis-related publications are "Soul-befriending, The Legacy of C.S. Lewis," *Spirituality* (Dublin; Vol. VI, No. 33. November–December 2000, 357–361); and eleven entries in *The C.S. Lewis Reader's Encyclopedia*, Jeffrey D. Schultz and John G. West, Jr., eds. (Grand Rapids: Zondervan, 1998).

Dr. Ford was a student for the Roman Catholic priesthood for twelve years. Rather than being ordained, he became a Benedictine monk at St. Andrew's Abbey, Valyermo, where he was for five years. The monastery sent him to be the first Roman Catholic doctoral student in the school of theology at Fuller Theological Seminary. The contemplative monks discerned that he had a call to be an active teacher, so Dr. Ford left monastic life and began teaching at Fuller where, for ten years, he was teaching assistant to the dean of the school of theology and lecturer in New Testament spirituality and in the theology of C.S. Lewis.

Since 1988 Dr. Ford has been teaching theology and liturgy at St. John's Seminary in Camarillo, California. He teaches courses on spirituality, church, sacraments, and liturgical music. His avocation is liturgical music. He is a member of the five-composer team, the Collegeville Composers Group, who are producing *Psallite: Sacred Songs for Liturgy and Life* (Collegeville: The Liturgical Press, 2005, 2006 and 2007). He had published *By Flowing Waters: Chant for the Liturgy* (Collegeville, MN: Liturgical Press, 1999), a CD: *By Flowing Waters: Chant for the Liturgy: A Selection of 25 Chants* (Collegeville, MN: Liturgical Press, 1999), and *Lord, By Your Cross and Resurrection: The Chants of By Flowing Waters for Holy Week and Easter Sunday*, Booklet (Fifty-four chants) and double CD (Sixty-eight chants [51 tracks]) (Collegeville, MN: Liturgical Press, 2001). He is married to Dr. Janice Daurio who received her doctorate in philosophy from the Claremont Graduate School. They make their home in Camarillo, California.

END NOTES

1. C.S. Lewis, "On Criticism," *Of Other Worlds: Essays and Stories*, Walter Hooper, ed. (New York: Harcourt, Brace and World, 1966) 57 (Lewis's emphasis).

2. The dictionaries tell us that to appreciate is to make or form an estimate of worth, quality or amount, to perceive the full force of, or to esteem adequately or highly, to recognize as valuable or excellent, or to find worth in.

3. Jeffrey D. Schultz and John G. West, Jr., eds. (Grand Rapids, Michigan: Zondervan, 1998): Balfour, Arthur James; Books of Influence; Chronicles of Narnia; The Horse and His Boy; The Last Battle; The Lion, the Witch and the Wardrobe; MacDonald George; The Magician's Nephew; Prince Caspian, The Silver Chair; The Voyage of the DAWN TREADER, q.v.

4. C.S. Lewis, "Sometimes Fairy Stories May Say Best What's to Be Said," *Of Other Worlds: Essays and Stories*, 37.

5. There are so many editions that I refer you to the fifth full paragraph.

6. The 1994 HarperCollins hard-and-soft-cover trade editions and the mass-market paperback edition.

7. Walter Hooper, C.S. *Lewis: A Companion and Guide* (New York: HarperCollins, 1996) 452 and 454. Hooper makes available a few of the first British reviews on 449-450.

8. *Reading with the Heart: The Way into Narnia* (Grand Rapids, Michigan: Eerdmans, 1979).

9. Roger Lancelyn Green and Walter Hooper, C.S. *Lewis: A Biography* (London: Collins, 1974) 245.

10. See my entry, "Chronicles of Narnia," in *The C.S. Lewis Readers' Encyclopedia*. Schultz and West, eds. (Grand Rapids, Michigan, Zondervan, 1998).

11. 1858-1924. In the *Oxford Companion to English Literature* (1985) Margaret Drabble tells us: "She is remembered…for her children's books, tales of everyday family life sometimes mingled with magic. In 1898 her first stories about the young Bastables appeared with such success that she published three 'Bastable' novels in quick succession: *The Story of the Treasure-Seekers* (1899), *The Wouldbegoods* (1901), and *The New Treasure-Seekers* (1904). Other well known titles with a lasting appeal include *Five Children and It* (1902), *The Phoenix and the Carpet* (1904), *The Railway Children* (1906), and *The Enchanted Castle* (1907)."

12. It is significant that the child heroes of *The Magic City* and "The Aunt and Amabel" have their respective experiences in imaginary worlds in order to help them repair relationships they have damaged, Philip Haldane with his stepsister Lucy and Amabel (no last name given) with her great aunt.

13. Green and Hooper, 238.

14. Who can miss seeing the long evenings of a Northern Ireland summer in the following (p. 204 in the 1994 hardcover and trade paperback editions)? "But before [Tirian] had had much time to think of this he felt two strong arms thrown about him and felt a bearded kiss on his cheeks and heard a well remembered voice saying: 'What lad? Art thicker and taller since I last touched thee!' It was his own father, the good King Erlian: but not as Tirian had seen him last when they brought him home pale and wounded from his fight with

the giant, nor even as Tirian remembered him in his later years when he was a grayheaded warrior. This was his father, young and merry, as he could just remember him from very early days when he himself had been a little boy playing games with his father in the castle garden at Cair Paravel, just before bedtime on summer evenings. The very smell of the bread-and-milk he used to have for supper came back to him."

15. Chapter sixteen, "The Hunting of the White Stag," ninth full paragraph. For a more extensive discussion of Edmund's character and development, please see Edmund Pevensie in *Companion to Narnia*.

16. Edmund's excitement over "snakes" and Susan's excitement over "rabbits" in the British version for "foxes" in the American foreshadow Edmund's fall into evil and Susan's fall into vanity. Due to trade and union regulations at the time, all the Chronicles of Narnia were type-set first in England and then all over again in the United States; Lewis had to correct two different sets of galleys and made changes at that time. See "Variants" in "Using the Companion" in all but the first edition of *Companion to Narnia*.

17. A typographical error persists from the very first editions to the latest. When Mr. Beaver calls his wife and the children from the hiding place to see Father Christmas, he says, "come out, Sons and Daughters of Adam," when there is only one Son of Adam, Peter, there.

18. Chapter twelve, "Peter's First Battle," eighth full paragraph.

19. Rudolf Otto, *The Idea of the Holy: An Inquiry into the Non-rational Factor in the Idea of the Divine and its Relation to the Rational*, John W. Harvey, tr. (Oxford: Oxford, 1923). Lewis identified it as one of his "top ten" in *The Christian Century* 79:23 (June 6, 1962), 719.

20. How much this simile is like the one in the all American editions of what used to be in the eleventh full paragraph from chapter twelve, "The Dark Island," of *The Voyage of the **Dawn** Treader*, now disappeared from all further editions: "And just as there are moments when simply to lie in bed and see the daylight pouring through your window and to hear the cheerful voice of an early postman or

milkman down below and to realize that *it was only, a dream: it wasn't real*, is so heavenly that it was very nearly worth having the nightmare in order to have the joy of walking; so they all felt when they came out of the dark."

21. The summary statement found in chapter sixteen, "The Hunting of the White Stag," twenty-first full paragraph.

22. The HarperCollins Classroom Activity Guide to the Chronicles of Narnia, page three of the PDF file at www.narnia.com

23. "His last visitor was Kaye Webb, editor of Puffin Books in which *The Chronicles of Narnia* were appearing. 'We had a nice talk on Wednesday,' she wrote to Green, who had arranged the meeting. 'What a very great and dear man. How I wish I'd had a chance to know him well, but how grateful I am that you "introduced" us to each other. He promised to re-edit the books (connect the things that didn't tie up) and he asked me to come again...'" Green and Hooper, 307.

24. In Hooper, *C.S. Lewis: A Companion and Guide*, 426.

25. The last edition is in David Mills, *C.S. Lewis and the Art of Witness* (Grand Rapids, Michigan: Eerdmans, 1998), 185-202.

26. *C.S. Lewis: His Literary Achievement* (New York: St Martin's Press, 1987), 124-125 and *The Chronicles of Narnia: The Patterning of a Fantastic World* (New York: Twayne Publishers [Twayne Masterwork Studies No. 127], 1993), 111-115.

27. *Reading with the Heart: The Way into Narnia* (Grand Rapids, Michigan: Eerdmans, 1979) and "Elusive Birds and Narratives Nets: The Appeal of Story in C.S. Lewis's Chronicles of Narnia" in Andrew Walker and James Patrick, eds., *A Christian for All Christians: Essays in Honour of C.S. Lewis* (New York: Regnery Gateway, 1992), 116-131.

28. Dunbar is the granddaughter of Maureen Moore, Lady Dunbar of Hempriggs. She wrote her 1998 senior dissertation at Scotland's St. Andrew's University on the subject; its title is "The Wardrobe or the Rings? What is the best way to read C.S. Lewis's The Chronicles of Narnia: canonical or chronological?"

29. *Reading with the Heart*, 143.

30. For 1982; this calendar and the one for 1983 on Prince Caspian was intended to be a seven-year project of the Lewis estate and the Episcopal Radio-TV Foundation.

Family Connections

HELEN JOY LEWIS

By Douglas Gresham

Editor's note: On April 23, 1956 C.S. Lewis married Helen Joy Davidman Gresham by civil ceremony in a registry office in Oxford. Douglas is her son.

Any work about Jack (C.S. Lewis) would be sadly incomplete without considerable reference to his wife, and it is here indeed that some contemporary writers fall down. Some people find it difficult to accept that Jack did eventually marry, that the marriage was one of passionate love, that the marriage was complete in every way, and that it was perhaps the most important thing that Jack ever did for himself. If one wishes to look for the influences which his wife had upon him, one need look no further than the book he wrote with her help. *Till We Have Faces: A Myth Retold* is unlike anything else from his pen, and is the book that he regarded as his best. Both *A Grief Observed* (obviously) and *Letters to Malcolm: Chiefly on Prayer* show the profound influence which his wife had upon him. How was it then that a man of such astonishing intellectual prowess should be so changed by a mere few years of acquaintance and association with any one person?

To start to answer that question one would have to look carefully at the lives of both Jack and Joy, and this has already been done by many biographers, some very good and some very bad. Of the biographies, Joy is best studied in *And God Came In: The Extraordinary*

Story of Joy Davidman—Her Life and Marriage to C.S. Lewis by Lyle W. Dorsett (Macmillan) and Jack by George Sayer in his book *Jack: C.S. Lewis and His Times* (Harper and Row). I propose to look briefly at their backgrounds, and then try to relate how the two came together in a union which was remarkable for the depth of their love for each other and for their understanding of that love.

The hypocrisy which abounded in Oxford society in the early 1950s is well documented and needs but a mention. Women were not wholly welcomed into academic circles. They were neither expected nor accepted in the close-knit circles of men who prided themselves on their learning and philosophical understanding. Women were not expected to be the intellectual equals of their menfolk, and if they were, they were expected to have the good manners not to reveal the fact. Jack had always been one who stood aside from fashion. It was unfashionable to be a muscular and outspoken Christian and yet he was. It was unfashionable to accept that a man with a cockney accent might be as learned as one who spoke with an Oxbridge drawl, and yet Jack welcomed Charles Williams. It was a time when Americans were unpopular in England, and also generally regarded as having little to offer as young and upstart colonials, and yet Jack always judged them on their own merits. It was unfashionable to accept a woman on equal terms with men in the fields of academic prowess, and yet Jack welcomed Mrs. Joy Gresham into his circle as one who was able to debate with the best of them. Jack was isolated from the fashions of the day by his own intellectual ability and so wide an education that the foibles of fashion became of no account to him.

Joy grew up in an environment where she was encouraged to speak out and have her say—an environment in which women were more than ready to engage in debate with men, and scenting victory, would relentlessly close in for the kill. She too had the most amazing intellectual abilities, and largely because of them suffered the same kind of enislement that Jack had experienced all his life. Her intelligence was so high that when her father, who was a high school principal, tried to measure her IQ he found that it went off the scale. Something of an infant prodigy, she attained success in her university career at an early age, being one of the youngest graduates from her college. She plunged at once into the world to see not what it could do for her, but what she could do for it. Her early days as poet, journalist and novelist won her some small acclaim, and her marriage and two sons presented her with both joys and agonies. All of these things furthered her knowledge and forged her will. By 1952 she had written and published a book that is now regarded by many as a minor classic and is still in print and selling more that forty years later. *Smoke on the Mountain: An Interpretation of the Ten Commandments* (Westminster Press, 1953, 1954) is the book for which she is most remembered.

If there are two people who are, by a shared peculiarity (in this case vastly superior intellects), separated from the bulk of mankind, and those two people meet, it is almost certain that one of two things will occur. Either they will become rivals, or they will become very close friends. If they are both men, perhaps the first is most likely, and maybe also if they are both women, but in this case one was a man and the other was a woman, and thus the friendship that grew between them was almost completely inevitable. In today's rather idiotic world, Western society has reversed the order in which relationships should develop to lead to marriage. Today we expect young people to "fall in love" and then marry, oft times without ever really even knowing each other. What should happen is that *agape* should be the first basis for any relationship between two people, followed by *philia*, which in time gives rise to *storge*, and then and only then should *eros* be permitted to play a hand. It is exactly this structure that Jack and Joy's relationship followed. First there was simply the reaching out of two people towards each other in the love of God. This led to the development of a friendship, followed by the building of familiarity between them and at last they "fell in love." The love between them developed and deepened despite all that the devil could do to prevent it, and was still growing at the time of her death.

When Joy and Jack were first "married" it is debatable whether there was anything between them other than a loving friendship, and the marriage, as has been discussed elsewhere, was little more than an act of friendship in itself. Neither Jack nor Joy accepted that a civil marriage was of any validity outside of the requirements of bureaucracy. But when Joy was discovered to be suffering from a terminal cancer condition, Jack was brought face-to-face with the imminent and inevitable loss of someone who had become very much more to him than he had perhaps realized. Jack was compelled to face the fact that he loved her with far more than simply a combination of *agape, storge* and *philia*; that there was another love here to which he was a complete stranger. He was brought up all standing with the realisation that what he was encountering was the great emotional force of which poets have sung for millennia. Jack suddenly knew that he had fallen in love. He found for the first time in his life that the songs of the great poets were true. At last he could begin to understand Launcelot, as well as Arthur.

This was the beginning of the complete maturation of him as a man. He loved and knew he was losing. He plunged willingly into the agony of Calvary from the other point of view, that of the Father. By God's great mercy and grace, he was given a few short years in which to revel in his new found experience of complete love, a love which combined all the four elements and to which he learnt to add the fifth component, the loving of doing, the love of action. He became all at one time, a husband and father, a nurse and companion, a lover and friend to perhaps the one woman in the world who was his intellectual equal.

Joy too found the depth of her love for him in a sudden flash of realisation. That Joy loved him as a dependable friend is in no doubt at all. She too had grown to love him in *agape, philia* and *storge*, and his help and caring were her salvation in this time when she was so alone and in pain and fear. But suddenly his enormous love for her broke through the reserve that she had held around herself like a shield, and she was carried breathlessly into a dimension of love that perhaps few of us ever even experience. It happened in one flashing moment, and in that moment the two of them became as one. As time passed, and Jack devoted himself to her, she too returned his love by providing him with the strength that he needed to withstand the terrors and the pains that her illness held for him. Putting aside her own physical agony and her fear, she talked with him, encouraged him, loved him. By the virtue of her own strength and courage she held his head above the waters of fear and the darkness of despair. Together they enjoyed the life of the world around them; she showed

Jack how to see things differently, how to treasure the glory of a flower, the joy of stillness. Joy taught Jack how to look at the world in a new light, the light that shared love brings to one's consciousness. And then, she died. What contribution did Joy make to Jack in their marriage? She completed him; she taught him love.

DOUGLAS H. GRESHAM

Douglas Howard Gresham was born on November 10, 1945, in the city of New York, the second son of novelist, William Lindsay Gresham (1909-62), and the poet/novelist, Helen Joy Davidman (1915-60). After the publication of his father's *Nightmare Alley* in 1946, the family moved to Ossining, New York, and then to Staatsburg. It was not long afterwards, however, that marital problems began, and in 1952 his mother spent several months in England completing her book, *Smoke on the Mountain: An Interpretation of the Ten Commandments* (1953). While there she became friends with C.S. Lewis and spent Christmas with the Lewis brothers in Oxford. After breaking with William Gresham, his mother returned to England in 1953 with her sons. Their first home was London.

Following his parents' divorce in 1954, Douglas went to school in Surrey. The next year the family moved to Headington, Oxford. In 1956 his mother and Lewis were married in a civil ceremony, which was shortly followed, after the discovery of her terminal cancer condition, by a Christian marriage. After his mother died of the cancer in 1960, Douglas continued to live with Lewis in their Headington Quarry home until Lewis's death in 1963.

For the next few years, Douglas studied Agriculture, and worked on farms, and during this time he met and fell in love with Meredith ("Merrie") Conan-Davies. Douglas and Merrie were married on February 20, 1967, and shortly after the wedding, he and Merrie sailed for Australia. Over the many and eventful years they spent in Australia he was a farmer, a radio and televison broadcaster, a restauranteur, and many other things between. It was there in Australia that their children were born: James in 1968, Timothy in 1969, Dominick in 1971, and Lucinda in 1976. In 1990 they adopted Melody, then five years old, from Korea.

Since 1973 Douglas Gresham has worked with all aspects of the Estate of C.S. Lewis, is the Creative and Artistic Director of the C.S.Lewis Company, and Co-Producer of *The Lion, The Witch and The Wardrobe* movie. In 1993 the family moved to Ireland so that he could give more of his attention to his C.S. Lewis-related work. He has many other interests, as well. He and his wife, both of whom are committed Christians, have made their home in County Carlow, Ireland, a multi-faceted non-denominational Christian House Ministry. Specializing in counseling ministry and seminar hosting, they are kept very busy. In 1988 Douglas published his autobiographical book, *Lenten Lands: My Childhood With Joy Davidman and C.S. Lewis*, and in 2005 his biography of C.S. Lewis, *Jack's Life: The Life Story of C.S. Lewis*. He now works full time for the C.S. Lewis Company, and devotes his spare time to a variety of Christian work, which includes Christian teaching and lecturing, devotional writing, and together with Merrie, their in-house ministry of Christian hospitality devoted to addressing whatever work the Lord sends them.

W.H. Lewis: Popular Historian

By Charles J. Wrong

arren Hamilton Lewis, as no doubt all readers know, was C.S. Lewis's only sibling. He was a regular officer in the British army, a career he did not much enjoy. He retired in 1932 with the rank of captain, was recalled to service in the Second World War with the temporary rank of major, was in the evacuation from Dunkirk, and was invalided out in August 1940. The lifelong intimate friend of his younger brother, he survived him by ten years, dying in 1973 at the age of seventy-seven.

A review of one of his books in *The New Yorker* referred to him as "C.S. Lewis's worldly brother." It is not clear what, if anything, the reviewer meant by the adjective. Unlike "Jack" Lewis, "Warnie" never wrote specifically on the subject of religion; but it is quite clear from his writings that his religious beliefs were the same as his brother's. As it happens, the two brothers were re-converted at about the same time, but independently of each other.

Warren Lewis early developed a lifelong interest in French history, particularly the seventeenth and early eighteenth centuries. He was not, like his brother, a scholar; but he had an inquiring mind, and his writing style, like his brother's, was very readable. He set out to become a historian of the *Grand Siècle*, the "great age" of French history. This period is usually taken to coincide with the personal rule of Louis XIV (1661-1715). Some would put its beginning earlier than that; but that anyone would put its end later seems improbable.

Warnie knew French, of course. How well he knew it is hard to say; he spelled *Chartres* with a circumflex accent, which would have raised French eyebrows. However, his knowledge of French history was extensive. His first and best book, *The Splendid Century: Life in the France of Louis XIV*, covers a wide range of very diverse fields. And he is always careful to help us keep track of the people he's talking about. The first mention of anyone's name is almost invariably accompanied by a footnote, giving us his or her full name and titles, dates of birth and death, and a one-sentence comment on their character.

The fact that he is prepared to sum up so many people with one sentence each suggests that his judgments are inclined to be a little too pat. Though wide, his knowledge of French history was not exactly deep. Historians know that the problems of the past, as of the present, are rarely simple, even when we know all the facts; which, when dealing with the France of three centuries ago, we don't. Lewis as a historian believed that issues of true or false, right or wrong, wise or foolish, feasible or impracticable, were clear-cut. He was also inclined to be much too simplistic in passing judgment on individuals. His portraits of Louis XIV and his nephew, the Duke of Orleans, are thoughtful and balanced, but he takes no such trouble with anyone else. For example, he dismisses Richelieu, Mazarin and Louis XIII as bad characters with no redeeming qualities, and is convinced that Louis XIII was nothing but Richelieu's helpless and bitterly resentful puppet. Historians in general agree that there was far more even to Louis XIII than that, and Lewis's thumbnail sketches of the two cardinals are mere caricatures. On the other hand, he gives Charles II of England credit for much too much shrewdness, and Louise de la Valliere (probably) far too much for selfless devotion. And we need to be equally sceptical, in all probability, about his comments on all the minor characters.

The Splendid Century appeared in 1953. It was an immediate smash hit, as it fully deserved to be, and has remained popular ever since. Each of his other books dealt with a single subject (in fact, essentially with a single man); but this book ranged over a number of fields, though by no means covering the whole picture. Lewis had been working on the book for some years. One chapter, dealing with the galley fleet and the living conditions of its rowers, had appeared in a *festschrift* entitled, *Essays Presented to Charles Williams*, published in 1947. The preface, by his brother, C.S. Lewis, says, "My brother's lifelong interest in the reign of Louis XIV was a bond between Williams and him which no one had foreseen when they first met." (Williams's own interest in the period does not seem to have found expression in any of his published work. At any rate, I have read most of it, and can't remember any reference to the France of the *Grand Siècle*.)

W.H. Lewis's style can be judged from a couple of quotations from this book. "Life on board while the galley was at sea was a sort of Hell's picnic, for there was really no accommodation for anyone.... Cooking facilities were primitive, and, as no one ever washed, the ship crawled with vermin from stem to stern." (Readers of C.S. Forester's *Mr. Midshipman Hornblower* will remember his description of what it was like to find yourself downwind of a galley.) And "The only prominent fish eater by choice was the Duc de Vendôme, and he preferred it stale to fresh and stinking to stale, a perversity of taste which ultimately killed him."

Now that he had got started as an historian of seventeenth century France, Lewis went on to publish a number of other books in the same field. In 1958 appeared *Assault on Olympus: The Rise of the House of Gramont between 1604 and 1678*, the story of the rise to eminence of the Gascon family of de Gramont. This is really just the biography of one member of that family: Antoine who, in a life of some seventy-four years, rose to be a duke and Marshal of France, and turned the Gramonts from obscure and impoverished Gascon nobility into one of the great houses of France. The book suffers, not only from its concentration on one family (and a handful of individuals in that family), but from Lewis's obvious dislike of Gascons in general and Gramonts in particular. It would be interesting to ascertain the opinions, both on the family and the book, of the well-known biographer who started out as Sanche de Gramont. He seems to have renounced his pedigree, as he moved to the United States and changed his name to Ted Morgan. This is an anagram of de Gramont—he appears to have discarded the Sanche.

In 1959, Lewis brought out a much better book, *Louis XVI: An Informal Portrait*. This is a simple popular biography, but it presents a balanced, thoughtful, and fairly convincing picture of Louis. The author has a good deal of sympathy with his subject, and this makes for a much more interesting book than the previous one; it is difficult for an author to sustain his readers' interest in a character he himself dislikes. The king receives credit where credit is due (sometimes where British historians have failed to allow him any), but this is no work of hagiography (as are, for instance, most books by British historians on Queen Elizabeth I). Full attention is paid to Louis's numerous shortcomings, and major crimes against humanity, such as the devastation of the Palatinate and the revocation of the Edict of Nantes, are sternly denounced. And the book is as readable as all Lewis's books were.

In 1961 appeared *The Scandalous Regent: A Life of Phillipe, Duc d'Orléans 1674-1723 and of His Family*. Philippe was Louis XIV's nephew, and Regent of France from Louis XIV's death in 1715 until he himself died in 1723. (New Orleans is named after him, and he was the ancestor of France's last king, Louis-Philippe.) In his earlier books Lewis had portrayed the Regent in a thoroughly unsympathetic light. He had allowed that he was "a blackguard but not a cad," which I find rather a subtle distinction; but that was about as far as he was prepared to go in his favour. Now that he was writing a full-length book about him, however, he drew the Regent as basically a sympathetic character, with many likeable and some admirable qualities. He brought out Philippe's skill and courage as a soldier (qualities that, Lewis admitted, his otherwise deplorable father had also possessed); his generosity and kindness, especially to children; his good nature and refusal to seek revenge or bear grudges. No longer a blackguard (whatever Lewis originally meant by that word), Philippe is now seen as a remarkably gifted man, whose gifts bore little or no fruit because of his laziness, and his insistence on gratifying his sensual appetites. Just exactly what went on behind closed doors at what the old history books used to call "nameless orgies," Lewis doesn't tell us. Probably he didn't know;

probably nobody but the participants ever knew. It seems clear, though, that the Regent's sins were the kind that hurt nobody but the sinner himself. His real crime as ruler of France was his failure, through indolence, to do the good he might have done.

The next year, 1962, Lewis brought out *Levantine Adventurer: The Travels and Missions of the Chevalier d'Arvieux, 1653-1697*, an account of the travels of the Chevalier d'Arvieux in the Near East, in the second half of the seventeenth century. (I can't comment on this book, as I have been unable to obtain a copy of it.)

In 1963, Lewis brought out *The Sunset of the Splendid Century*. Disappointingly, this was not a sequel to his first book, *The Splendid Century: Life in the France of Louis XIV*. To some extent it overlapped it, for it was the biography of the Duc du Maine, one of Louis XIV's illegitimate children by Madame de Montespan.

In 1964, after his brother's death, W.H. Lewis published *Memoirs of the Duc de Saint-Simon*, famous as the friend of the Regent, the bitter enemy of Louis XIV, and the purveyor of innumerable fascinating but largely fictitious stories about his court. Incidentally, in *The Sunset of the Splendid Century* Lewis says the duke was the last of his house. He was mistaken, and it is rather an odd mistake for him to have made. He must surely have known about a later Saint-Simon, the Utopian Socialist, and it must have crossed his mind to wonder if they were related. As a matter of fact, they were. Before the Revolution the Utopian Socialist, like the duke before him, was a member of the court nobility and a colonel in the French army. Both had the same surname (de Rouvroy), so clearly the house survived well into the nineteenth century, whatever may have happened to it since.

Letters of C.S. Lewis was published in 1966. It was edited by Warren Lewis, who provided, in a twenty-six-page introduction, a brief biography of the man he called "the best of brothers and friends." This title, *Brothers and Friends: The Diaries of Major Warren Hamilton Lewis*, was used by Clyde S. Kilby and Marjorie Lamp Mead for their edition of Warren Lewis's diaries, an intimate portrait of C.S. Lewis, published in 1982, nine years after Warren's death.

The younger brother was the famous one. As a scholar, as a Christian apologist, as a writer of fiction, and simply as a man, C.S. Lewis is a major figure; a fact borne out by the number of people who still feel impelled to make vicious attacks on him. No one would call Warren Lewis a major figure in any capacity. Nevertheless, he was a good writer, with an attractive and highly readable style; and some of his books are worth keeping on your shelves. I would not part with my own copies of *Louis XVI: An Informal Portrait* and *The Scandalous Regent: A Life of Phillipe, Duc d'Orléans*, even though both books, especially the latter, devote far too much space to court intrigues and the real or pretended love affairs of the house of Bourbon.

But there can be no question about it: *The Splendid Century: Life in the France of Louis XIV* is a classic. It covers a wide variety of fields, and covers them very well. There is, of course, a chapter on the king, Louis XIV, and another on the court. The latter contains an excellent description of what life at Versailles, for a member of that court, was actually like. It is difficult to see how any of them could stand it. Saint-Simon had the best set of rooms (for non-royalty) in the chateau: "His quarters consisted of three small rooms, looking out on a stinking courtyard, an entrance hall and closets you could just stand upright, these spaces having been cut in two horizontally, to provide servants' cubicles." A courtier of less importance would be lucky "to be the possessor of a couple of matchboard cabins under the roof, hot in summer, cold in winter, in which he could not speak above a whisper without being overheard by his neighbours, and permanently fetid with the stench of the neighbouring latrines." As for the king himself, Lewis describes the appallingly protracted ritual which always had to be gone through before he got anything to eat; and wonders whether he ever tasted hot food, except when taking pot luck with his generals in the field.

The next chapter, "The Base of the Pyramid," tells us about the life of French peasants, with particular attention to the *Taille*, the infamous tax from which the privileged classes were exempt. He doesn't have a lot to tell us about peasant life (for that we have to go to historians like Goubert or Le Roy Ladurie), but what he does have to say is interesting. Other chapters deal with the church (and particularly the controversy with the Jansenists, and the theological battle between Bossuet and Fénelon); the army; the world of the country gentlemen who provided the officers for the army and navy; the prosperous bourgeoisie; the medical world (one wonders how any patient under a doctor's care ever survived); "the art of living," dealing primarily with good manners and food; the galleys (the chapter that appeared in the *festschrift*); long distance sea travel; the girls' school at St-Cyr founded by Madame de Maintenon; and the world of letters.

It is a great pity that Lewis did not extend his coverage to other fields, and prolong it into at least the first third of the eighteenth century. The title, *The Sunset of the Splendid Century*, seems to imply that the latter book would cover changes, for example, in the army, the church, daily life for all classes, and the world of letters, at the very least; and the changes in all these fields were important. But all the book does is focus on the Duc du Maine. And the trouble with the Duke is that he is now, and was then, an abysmal bore, a fact glaringly apparent to all his contemporaries except his father and his adoring stepmother. The "scandalous Regent" is by no means a bore, and must have been fascinating company as long as he remained sober; but the book about him has far too little to tell us of the France over which he ruled.

Even within the reign of Louis XIV there are a number of fields which Lewis could profitably have covered, instead of wandering off in pursuit of the Duc du Maine and the house of Gramont. Lewis deals with the army and the galleys, but not the "navy" proper, the warships that in Louis XIV's reign gave the English and Dutch navies a good run for their money. There is hardly anything about the great minister, Colbert, whose immense work of economic reconstruction is covered in two fat volumes by the historian C.W. Cole. It was in Louis XIV's reign that the French colonial empire was founded (Richelieu had been interested, but Mazarin had not); yet Lewis says practically nothing about it. We could also have done with a great deal more information about peasant life, the field so richly cultivated by Goubert. And, while Lewis has a chapter on female education (actually limited to St-Cyr), he tells us practically nothing about the education of boys, either at school or at the universities.Unfortunately, after that first delightful book, Lewis appears to have lost interest in covering the social, economic and cultural aspects of the period. But we do have *The Splendid Century*, and it's a classic.

CHARLES J. WRONG

Charles J. Wrong was a pupil of C.S. Lewis for one eight-week term in 1935. Freshmen were required to take an exam known as Pass Moderations, which included Political Science texts: Aristotle, Hobbes, Rousseau, de Tocqueville. Charles did not know of Lewis as a writer of Christian apologetics. The student found his tutor very impressive as a personality. The latter was always courteous and considerate, but an exacting and formidable tutor, who commanded the former's respect. Strangely, although Lewis knew who Charles's father was, and had liked and admired him, he never mentioned him to Charles.

While serving in Italy in 1944 Charles discovered Lewis as a Christian writer, from his books sent to him by relatives. He was impressed by *Perelandra (Voyage to Venus)* and *The Screwtape Letters*. Later he read his other books, including a couple in his professional field. Charles never thought of Lewis as a specifically Protestant writer, and the fact that he became a Roman Catholic in 1947 did not alter his growing enthusiasm for Lewis as a man and writer.

Charles visited Lewis in Oxford and was his guest for lunch in college. He ran into him twice later. The second meeting is described in "A Chance Meeting," his contribution to *C.S. Lewis at the Breakfast Table and Other Reminiscences*," edited by James T. Como. Charles knew Stephen Schofield, the founding publisher/editor of *The Canadian C.S. Lewis Journal*.

Sightings

"An Examiner's Nightmare"/ "Awake, My Lute!"

By Burton K. Janes

In June 1943, Edward Weeks (1898-1989), then editor of the thoughtful and stylish *Atlantic Monthly*, received a letter from Harold Butler of the British Embassy, informing him that the Ministry of Information was inviting a small number of American editors to observe the British war effort. Butler hoped Weeks could arrange to be one of the first quartet in early July. Space would be reserved for them on a British aircraft and they would be guests of the Ministry for six weeks.

Weeks accepted, pleased to learn that his companions would be Laurence Winship of the *Boston Globe*, Ralph McGill of the *Atlanta Constitution*, and Oliver C. Keller of the *Pittsburgh Post-Gazette*. In England, Weeks met several talented writers, including John Masefield (1878-1967), Barbara Ward (1914-81), and Osbert (1892-1969) and Edith (1887-1964) Sitwell. All of them became important contributors to the magazine Weeks edited.

Another talented writer Weeks met was C.S. Lewis, fellow and tutor in English Language and Literature at Magdalen College. The American editor purchased a poem by the Oxford don, thereby also attracting the latter as a contributor to the prestigious magazine devoted to literature, science, art and politics.

Weeks squeezed in the train for Oxford which was jam-packed with naval personnel, American airmen, and civilians. In Old Headington, Weeks stayed with Richard Creswick, a friend and the director of the Bodleian Library. Weeks told him of those he hoped to meet the following day: Salvador de Madariaga (1886-1978), the Spanish exile; Sir Richard Livingstone; C.S. Lewis; and Lord Elton. "My dear Weeks," Dick said, "you're doing a literary pub-crawl!"

Weeks, who had arrived in the midst of examinations, found Lewis "grubbing in his rose garden." The gardener rose and shook the editor's hand. "Stand by for a moment while I finish this job," he said. "Then we'll have a cup of tea." The job finished, they retired to Lewis's study which, Weeks recalled in *Writers and Friends*, was "a maze of books and papers." Weeks also wrote in his memoir, "Lewis was too evangelistic for Oxford; they looked down their noses at his popular books, *The Screwtape Letters* and its more spiritual successor, *The Problem of Pain*, but his following had grown."

Weeks asked, "What are you up to?"

"At the moment, nothing but the Examinations; they squeeze one dry."

Weeks spied a handwritten poem on Lewis's desk. "Is that yours?" the editor asked.

"Oh, some giddy verses I wrote when I couldn't sleep, 'An Examiner's Nightmare.' Do read it."

Weeks did. It began, "I stood in the gloom of a spacious room...." He then bought the manuscript and carted it off, with the promise that Lewis would show the Atlantic Monthly Press chapters of his next book, presumably *Beyond Personality*, which was published in 1944 by Geoffrey Bles and in 1945 by Macmillan of New York.

At the end of their six-week English jaunt and before boarding the seaplane in Poole Harbour, the Americans were examined by Customs. "Will you open your bags, please." Customs began to puzzle over the baffling contents of Weeks's briefcase, which included a Mongolian drinking cup, a silver brooch, Liberty scarves, and C.S. Lewis's handwritten comic poem. The latter might perhaps be in code, despite Weeks's protest that it was written by an evangelical Oxford don. It was set aside, together with an article by Sir William Beveridge (1879-1963). They would be read and mailed to Weeks if cleared. The tax, when figured, embarrassed Weeks, but a Canadian officer, who had been waiting patiently in line, apprised the situation and lent Weeks the requisite £5.

On his same trip to England, Weeks also acquired the annual Shakespeare lecture of the British Academy, *Hamlet, The Prince or the Poem?*, which C.S. Lewis delivered in 1942 (reprinted in *They Asked for a Paper: Papers and Addresses* and *Selected Literary Essays*). "Here," Weeks commented in *The Atlantic Monthly*, "is criticism penetrating and of such spiritual elevation that as you read it the anxiety of war fades from mind."

C.S. Lewis's poem, "An Examiner's Nightmare," was renamed "Awake, My Lute!" and published in *The Atlantic Monthly* in 1943 (reprinted in *The Collected Poems of C.S. Lewis*). Chad Walsh (1914-91), the author of the first book about Lewis, *C.S. Lewis: Apostle to the Skeptics*, writes: "The one poetic genre in which [Lewis] excels is adult nonsense verse. Here he rivals Lewis Carroll. It is regrettable that he has not written more of his delightful jingles, and that to locate the few in print requires a painful search through magazine files." Walsh dubs "Awake, My Lute!" as "one of [Lewis's] few completely successful poems," which he then quotes in its entirety. Walter Hooper claims that Lewis's "delightful nonsense poem" was "inspired by the Lord Chancellor's nightmare" in *Iolanthe*, one of the series of famous popular comic operas written by Gilbert and Sullivan ("When you're lying awake with a dismal headache, and repose is taboo'd by anxiety..."). Don W. King suggests, "The key to understanding this concoction of incoherent revelries concerning boring lecturers, shipmates on the Ark, and insufficient answers on Oxford examinations is they are the disconnected fragments of a dream."

Lewis's work appeared again in *The Atlantic Monthly*, with the publication of "The Efficacy of Prayer" in 1959 (reprinted in *The World's*

Last Night And Other Essays and *Fern-seed and Elephants And Other Essays on Christianity*). By then, Lewis must have, in Chad Walsh's words, "wisely reconciled himself to his inherent limitations as a poet, and chose to say extremely well in prose what he could only stammer in verse." Still, "Awake, My Lute!" remains a gem. Lewis concludes his poem, "And the bed of that sea was my bed." The poem is so delightful, one wishes the poet had not awakened so quickly from his dream!

WORKS CITED

- *Iolanthe*. Gilbert and Sullivan opera, 1882.

- King, Don W. "Awake, My Lute!" In *The C.S. Lewis Readers' Encyclopedia*. Eds., Jeffrey D. Schultz and John G. West, Jr. Grand Rapids, MI. Zondervan Publishing House, 1998.

- ——. Personal correspondence.

- Lewis, C.S. "Awake, My Lute!" *The Atlantic Monthly*. 172 (November 1943): 113, 115.

- ——. *The Collected Poems of C.S. Lewis*. Ed., Walter Hooper. London: Fount, 1994.

- ——. "The Efficacy of Prayer." *The Atlantic Monthly*. 188 (January 1959): 59-61.

- ——. *Fern-seed and Elephants And Other Essays on Christianity*. Ed., Walter Hooper. London: Collins, Fontana, 1975.

- ——. "Hamlet: The Prince or the Poem?" *The Proceedings of the British Academy*, XXVIII. London: Oxford University Press, 1942.

- ——. *Selected Literary Essays*. Ed., Walter Hooper. Cambridge: Cambridge University Press, 1969.

- ——. *They Asked for a Paper: Papers and Addresses*. London: Geoffrey Bles, 1962.

- ——. *The World's Last Night And Other Essays*. New York: Harcourt, Brace and World, 1960.

- Walsh, Chad. C.S. *Lewis: Apostle to the Skeptics*. New York: The Macmillan Company, 1949.

- Weeks, Edward. "The Atlantic Bookshelf." *The Atlantic Monthly*. 172 (October 1943): 125.

- ———. *Writers and Friends*. Boston, MA: Atlantic-Little, Brown Books, 1981.

BOB JONES, JR. MEETS C.S. LEWIS

By Burton K. Janes

The meeting of Bob Jones, Jr. (1911-97), self-described as "an outspoken fundamentalist" (*Cornbread and Caviar* [Greenville, South Carolina: Bob Jones University Press, 1985], p. 66), with C.S. Lewis is documented elsewhere (see, for example, Roger Lancelyn Green and Walter Hooper, *C.S. Lewis: A Biography* [London: Collins, 1974], p. 229; Walter Hooper, "C.S. Lewis and C.S. Lewises," in *G.K. Chesterton and C.S. Lewis: The Riddle of Joy*, eds., Michael H. Macdonald and Andrew A. Tadie [Grand Rapids, Michigan: Eerdmans, 1989], p. 41; and *idem*, "C.S. Lewis: The Man and His Thought," in *Essays on C.S. Lewis and George MacDonald*, ed., Cynthia Marshall [Lewiston, New York: Edwin Mellen, 1991], p. 11).

Walter Hooper, who met Jones in 1954, asked him what he thought of Lewis. A severe look crossed Jones's face. "That man smokes a pipe," he said slowly, "and that man drinks liquor," he added, then after a pause said, "but I *do* believe he is a Christian." Jones's own recollection in recent years of his meeting with Lewis carries with it a strong lesson in tolerance and acceptance, and an attempt to understand an individual of a different theological persuasion.

Shortly after the Second World War, Jones and the Anglican bishop, the Reverend A.W. Goodman Hudson, were passing through

Oxford. Lewis and Goodman Hudson had been associated in some special activity during the war. Through Goodman Hudson,[1] Jones met Lewis, who came to lunch with them at the hotel there, either the Mitre or the public house, the Eagle and Child (popularly called the Bird and Baby).

While the trio was eating, Lewis drank about a pint of ale and smoked his pipe. "Of course," Jones wrote a correspondent in 1979, "it is very difficult for me to reconcile the pipe and the tankard of ale with a Christian testimony."

During their meal, Lewis spoke of his conversion. Then he expressed keen interest in the philosophical implications of how God answers prayer, a subject which led to a lengthy discussion, although in 1994 Jones could recall none of the details. Lewis also discussed the book—on prayer—that he was planning to write. Was it the same idea that came to fruition nearly two decades later as *Letters to Malcolm: Chiefly on Prayer*?

Following lunch, Lewis pushed his chair back and relit his pipe. "Which of my books do you like the best?" he asked Jones.

Rather apologetically, Jones said that Lewis's trilogy—*Out of the Silent Planet, Perelandra (Voyage to Venus)* and *That Hideous Strength: A Modern Fairy-Tale for Grown-Ups*—which he thought posed theological problems under the guise of science fiction, appealed to him more than anything else Lewis had written.

Clapping his hands, Lewis said, "Good show! Those are my own favourites."

Thirty-one years old, Jones had been tremendously impressed with *The Screwtape Letters* when it appeared in 1942. In the years after their meeting, Jones read more of Lewis's works and saw *Shadowlands* a couple of times (Jones to Janes, November 10, 1993).

"Lewis may not always have been orthodox," Jones commented in his autobiography, "but he was seldom dull." While he admits that his own impression of Lewis continued to be ambivalent, he identified him as an interesting writer because he "seemed to be especially gifted at making theology simple and setting forth theological truths in allegorical form." Among the reams of material written about Lewis since his death in 1963, Jones felt that "the 'New Evangelicals' seem to have embraced him as sort of a patron saint, and fundamentalists generally seem to shy away from him as a heretic." However, he concluded, "in conversation, he gave a very good personal testimony of his own faith in Christ."

Hooper thinks that the teetotaler Jones "learned something very valuable about the behaviour of not just one fellow Christian, but most of them. And it certainly had not led him to be bitter." That perhaps the most uncompromising fundamentalist in America at that time could meet the unconventional, broad-minded Anglican Lewis and accept him as a fellow believer gives hope to those of us who pray ardently for spiritual unity among believers if organic unity is not attainable. Any progress along these lines would serve to demolish what Lewis called "our tragic and sinful divisions" and replace them with a certain heavenly unity" (C.S. Lewis, *Christian Reunion and Other Essays*, ed., Walter Hooper [London: Collins, 1990], pp. 17, 21).

END NOTE

1. Goodman Hudson later went to Australia, where he assisted the Archbishop of Sydney. Returning to England, he pastored a church in London. He died several years ago.

C.S. LEWIS'S HONOURARY DEGREES

By Burton K. Janes

In the premiere issue of *The Canadian C.S. Lewis Journal*, founding editor Stephen L. Schofield recalled dining with W.H. ("Warnie") Lewis at the Mitre in Oxford in 1968. In the course of conversation, Warnie mentioned that his brother, C.S. Lewis, had "never travelled."

"Yes," Schofield said, "it's a pity. He never crossed the Atlantic, did he?"

"No," answered the Major, "but we nearly did once." That was in 1952 when Université Laval in Quebec bestowed an honourary degree on C.S. Lewis.

Schofield concluded his article with a note, "Perhaps it merits recording that no English or American university thus honoured Lewis, then at the peak of his renown. The only other to confer on him an honourary degree was St. Andrews University, Scotland."[1]

In the third issue of the journal, Graeme W.M. Muckart, then at St. Mary's College (University of St. Andrews), offered a correction: "in all...five, not two, universities 'thus honoured Lewis'—including one English one."[2] This article is a recapping of those honourary degrees.

University of St. Andrews (June 28, 1946). On April 8, 1946 the Senate resolved to confer the Honourary Degree of Doctor of Divinity upon the following individuals recommended by the Committee: Rev.

J.W. Arthur, Rev. Alexander Campsie, Rev. T.W. Gardiner, Rev. Dr. Josef Krenek and C.S. Lewis.

The Promoter was Professor D.M. Baillie, Dean of the Faculty of Divinity. The account of the laureation given in the local paper reads as follows:

> It is unnecessary to dwell upon Mr. Lewis's first class academic record in various fields of humane learning, nor will I speak much of his distinguished work as a literary critic, which I am not well qualified to assess, and which it would be impertinent to praise. It is because he has made striking contributions to the literature of religion that he stands before us in a place of honour today.
>
> But his work derives a peculiar interest from the fact that it is impossible to draw a clear line between his literary criticism and his divinity; the one flows into the other, and he has thus come to belong to the fine tradition of those literary critics who judge and write as they do because they know where they stand in relation to the ultimate problems and beliefs. *A Preface to Paradise Lost* is an illuminating introduction to Milton's great epic because it takes theology seriously.
>
> Both with his pen and with his voice on the radio, Mr. Lewis has succeeded in capturing the attention of many who will not readily listen to professional theologians and has taught them many lessons concerning the deep things of God. For such an achievement, which could only be compassed by a rare combination of literary fancy and religious insight, every Faculty of Divinity must be grateful. In recent years, Mr. Lewis has arranged a new kind of marriage between theological reflection and poetic imagination and this fruitful union is now producing works which are difficult to classify in any literary genre: it can only be said in respectful admiration that he pursues "things unattempted yet in prose or rhyme."
>
> It is not very frequently that the University confers its Doctorate of Divinity upon a lay theologian, but it may well

be proud to give this acknowledgement to the work of Mr. C.S. Lewis.[3]

Later that day, Warnie in his diary recalled strolling:

… into St. Mary's College. … Jack now noticed with concern … that all the bustling figures were wearing white ties; so we went across the road to one Fudyce, a draper, who to our relief let him buy a white collar and tie on a promise to post the coupons to him.

As we sat smoking a final cigarette in the hotel lounge, J, now correctly clad, remarked that this graduation business was the only regrettable feature in the holiday; and I agreed with him.

We already found quite a crowd at the Younger Hall, where the graduation ceremony was to take place, the undergraduates looking very well in their red gowns with fur trimmings. … When at last the dignitaries arrived, the girls struck up "The animals came in two by two … ," and among the "animals" was J, now clad in a black cassock with scarlet buttons, and with him twelve others in similar get up, the only one of whom I recognized being [pianist Dame] Myra Hess.

The actual ceremony was pretty, but tedious: difficult indeed to see how it could help being so, though some of the girl graduands were very pretty.… There were perhaps 70 or 80 degrees conferred, and then came the honouraries, of whom J was the last.

Each honourary recipient was the subject of a poorish eulogy, delivered not as at Oxford by the Public Orator, but by the Dean of the Faculty concerned.… Each recipient was handed a sort of tubular case containing his degree, and a great nuisance J was to find his on the journey until he could get it stowed in his suitcase.

I slipped out just at the moment when the Vice-Chancellor's announcement that he was going to cut out more of his speech was being given a hearty round of applause.... At 4:55 I picked up a taxi by arrangement and went round with it to St. Mary's where I found the Vice-Chancellor just showing J out from tea; he asked to be introduced to me, and chid me for not inviting myself to the meal, which I thought was uncommonly civil of him.

We had, very stupidly, thought of a quiet train journey...but of course the train was packed with graduates etc. "going down": but still, we had corner seats from which to get a last view of this town, for which I have conceived a very lively liking.[4]

Universitié Laval (September 22, 1952). On the occasion of the centenary of the founding of the university, an honourary degree (Letters) was bestowed upon Lewis. Nicole Toffoli, Coordinator of Public Relations, wrote me, "Our archives are unfortunately incomplete on that ceremony..., but we can presume that Professor Lewis was able to be present because our University does not bestow honourary degrees *in absentia*."[5]

However, according to Warnie, Lewis was *not* present for the occasion. He told Stephen Schofield that his brother "wanted to see Quebec. And when Laval University gave him that degree, we were all set to go one summer. But something happened—I forget what it was now—to prevent the trip."[6]

The University of Manchester (May 13, 1959). The Chancellor of the University, The Right Honourable The Earl of Woolton, conferred on Lewis the Degree of Doctor of Letters (*honoris causa*). The other recipients were Sir Vincent Ziani de Ferranti, Dr. Harold Willis Dodds, Lady Ewing, Sir William Henry Pilkington (Doctor of Laws), and Professor Sir James Gray (Doctor of Science).

The Presenter, Professor R.A.C. Oliver, said:

Universities are compelled by circumstance to make a virtue of economy. The practice of frugality is in any case appropriate in the conferment of academic honours. It is therefore with the warm glow of virtue that I invite you to make a single degree serve at one and the same time for a versatile man of letters, a notable theologian, and a pre-eminent teacher and scholar. In a package deal I present to you a living disproof of the popular fallacy which equates the don with the narrow-minded pedant.

A don he is, but no ineffectual one. For nearly thirty years he was an ornament of Magdalen and of Oxford; his pupils were fortunate, his lectures famous. Latterly he moved, no doubt in a missionary English. As a scholar he is distinguished beyond all others in his field by the extraordinary range of his knowledge, as well in other languages as in English, and by the penetrating brilliance of his insight. His major works of scholarship and criticism, on both medieval and modern literature, are among the most influential writings in their field. His gifts of narrative and exposition are the admiration of his readers. One of his chief pleasures is walking; but it is in his physical habits alone that he is pedestrian. One vehicle of criticism, however, he has always disdained: he has too much integrity ever to mount the band-wagon. The good rather than the fashionable has been his standard. He has indeed enjoyed de-bunking the de-bunkers, and no cause can be regarded as lost while he defends it.

His formidable pen has been wielded mightily in the service of the Queen of the Sciences. It is not common for theological writings to become best-sellers, but the combination of wit and wisdom has made *The Screwtape Letters* irresistible. Presented as a do-it-yourself manual of instruction for young devils, it could legitimately expect a ready sale among this numerous company, but it has appealed even more to those who are on the side of the angels.

In matters of controversy it is a joy to see such a "bonny fechter" at work. He quotes a saying of Confucius: "With those who follow a different Way it is useless to take counsel." But he clearly believes it is not useless to take up the cudgels, and he wields a pretty cudgel, though always a fair one. When he calls his opponent a "clod," a "trousered ape," or "an irremediable blockhead," he is always at pains to show that the epithets are strictly appropriate and indeed restrained.

The scholar I present has in his autobiography admitted to his "distaste for all that is public," to his "inaptitude for formality." Yet a fair-minded man, shrink as he may from praise, will not consider it unseemly that a University should give itself the pleasure of saluting profound scholarship and brilliance of mind. I shall however defer to his modesty to the extent of foregoing the pleasure of praising in detail his novels, his poems, his space fiction and his delightful works for children. Suffice it to say that through all their variety, as in his life itself, what stands out is indeed a man of parts but also, in a deeper sense, a whole man.[7]

The menu of the Founder's Day luncheon to honourary graduates, which was held before the ceremony, indicates that both Lewis and Sir Harry Pilkington replied to the toasts proposed by the Chancellor. Lewis sat between a Mrs. Dodds and The Lady Mayoress of Manchester.

The University of Dijon (Universitye de Bourgogne) [1962]. Marie-Claire Remoissent of the Service Relations Internationales wrote me, "Unfortunately we were unable to trace any records concerning the ceremony of Doctor *Honoris Causa* in 1962. We confirm that C.S. LEWIS was made Docteur *Honoris Causa* of the University of Burgundy."[8] The other recipients that year were Antonio Almela, Leon H. Dupriez, Ulf von Euler, Gilliard (first name unknown), Paul Guggenheim, Hermann Jahrreiss, Nicolas Kaldor, Oscar Lange, Marcel Renard and Giovahni Sansone.

The University of Lyon (1963). This university honoured C.S. Lewis by making him Docteur de l'Universite. Despite repeated attempts, no further information has been forthcoming on this honour.

Question: Did Lewis receive an honourary degree from Durham?[9] (There was some conjecture that Lewis did receive this degree. I posed the question to other scholars at the end of this essay when I first published it, but it remains unanswered, as do some things from Lewis's life.)

END NOTES

1. Stephen L. Schofield, "Laval University, Quebec," *The Canadian C.S. Lewis Journal*, 1 (January 1979), p. 3.

2. Graeme W.M. Muckart, letter to the editor, *ibid.*, 3 (March 1979), p. 10.

3. *St. Andrews Citizen*, June 29, 1946. Paragraph divisions have been added.

4. *Brothers and Friends: The Diaries of Major Warren Hamilton Lewis*, eds., Clyde S. Kilby and Marjorie Lamp Mead (New York: Harper & Row, 1982), pp. 190f. Paragraph divisions have been added.

5. Nicole Toffoli to Burton K. Janes, March 9, 1994.

6. Schofield, "Laval University, Quebec," p. 3.

7. R.A.C. Oliver, Presenter's speech, May 13, 1959.

8. Marie-Claire Remoissenet to Burton K. Janes, July 22, 1994. See also *Remise des Diplomes de Docteur Honoris Causa*, November 25, 1993.

9. Christopher W. Mitchell to Burton K. Janes, April 11, 1996.

A LITTLE-KNOWN C.S. LEWIS LETTER

By Burton K. Janes

*A*fter reading *Surprised by Joy: The Shape of My Early Life*, C.S. Lewis's autobiography, Mrs. Ray Garrett of Salt Lake City, Utah, wrote a letter to its author. Today, however, she cannot recall her precise question. On September 12, 1960, Lewis responded to her query:

> Dear Mrs. Garrett,
>
> As you can see from the book the whole lesson of my life has been that no "methods of stimulation" are of any lasting use. They are indeed like drugs—a stronger dose is needed each time and soon no possible dose is effective. We must not bother about thrills at all. Do the present duty—*bear* the present pain—*enjoy* the present pleasure—and leave emotions and "experiences" to look after themselves. That's the programme, isn't it?
>
> With all good wishes,
>
> Yours sincerely
>
> C.S. Lewis[1]

Reading Lewis's letter for the first time in 1992, my initial thought was that he might have been thinking of his wife, Joy, who had died on July 13 of that year. Maybe the letter was a foretaste of his later book, *A Grief Observed*—barely being able to make it through the days by doing only what had to be done, bearing the ever-present pain, and enjoying the fleeting pleasures of life.

However, my hasty interpretation of the letter was quickly tempered by the responses of various individuals who studied it at my request. The late Stephen L. Schofield, founding editor of *The Canadian C.S. Lewis Journal*, thought the letter to be a typical Lewis statement, rather like his quoting George MacDonald, who always lived in "the holy Present."[2]

The late Sheldon Vanauken suggests that while Lewis indeed knew in 1960 the full meaning of "*bear* the present pain," he might very well have written that entire sentence at any time in the previous decade. Lewis knew very well that many past religions (eg., that of Isis or the pagan gods of Rome) and many contemporary churches sought to bring people to an emotional "high," which, in the end, drained them and failed to stimulate. Vanauken draws attention to Lewis's account of going into the garden to pray and being overwhelmed by the beauty and freshness—and later going into the garden to be overwhelmed, and not being. "Do your duty, and take what God gives," Vanauken interprets the letter. Lewis "believed that before the terrible pain of Joy's death, and said it or implied it to me in my deep grief." He may have also said or implied it to the "American Lady," who poured out her many woes, great and small, to him. While it is "a good, succinct letter," Vanauken feels it contains no "new insight through his bereavement."[3]

Peter Kreeft characterizes the letter as "typical, vintage Lewis." He elaborates:

> It urges his usual objective and self-forgetful rather than subjective and self-regarding attitude—old-fashioned, simple, common-sense, pre-modern wisdom, increasingly eroded as the "therapeutic" model of religion replaces the prophetic. But it is the teaching of all the saints—detachment from "sensible

consolations"—and foretaste of and training for the ecstatic self-forgetfulness of Heaven, of which the mystics show us an appetizer.

Kreeft suggests that Lewis would rather like the Chinese Christian parable, attributed to Watchman Nee, of the trio of men—Faith, Fact and Feeling, in that order—walking along a wall. As long as Faith keeps his eyes on Fact, all three walk on the wall. But when Faith turns around to see how Feeling is doing, he and Feeling both fall off the wall. Kreeft's summary of Lewis's letter? "Better advice than libraries of ingrown eyeball therapy."[4]

Walter Hooper, while calling the letter "very good," hopes I won't feel he is less enthusiastic than he should be when, like the late Stephen Schofield, he says it is really very typical of many Lewis wrote. Rather than being a foretaste of A Grief Observed, Hooper sees it as:

> ... something he had learned long ago when he made mistakes about the object of "Joy." It might almost be said that one of the things Lewis distrusted most was *thrills*. Apparently this distrust of thrills went hand in hand with his advice to enjoy present blessings and endure miseries. We get this early on in his writings.[5]

For example, in his first book, *The Pilgrim's Regress: An Allegorical Apology for Christianity, Reason and Romanticism*, Lewis uses thrill as a synonym for "desire," and there is even in Book II a city named Thrill. In the chapter, "Archetype and Ectype" he has a character say,

> You must fear thrills, but you must not fear them too much. It is only a foretaste of that which the real Desirable will be when you have found it.... Do you not know how it is with love? First comes delight: then pain: then fruit. And then there is joy of the fruit, but that is different again from the first delight, and mortal lovers must not try to remain at the first step: for lasting passion is the dream of a harlot and from it we wake in despair. You must not try to keep the raptures: they have done their work.[6]

There is also No. 15 of *The Screwtape Letters* where Screwtape says that the Enemy (God) would have us "obeying the present voice of conscience, bearing the present cross, receiving the present grace, giving thanks for the present pleasure."[7]

The "thrill" business also comes up in the chapter on "Christian Marriage" in *Mere Christianity*, where Lewis says,

> ... no feeling can be relied on to last in its full intensity, or even to last at all. Knowledge can last, principles can last, habits can last; but feelings come and go.... [I]t is just the people who are ready to submit to the loss of the thrill and settle down to the sober interest, who are then most likely to meet new thrills in some quite different direction.... Let the thrill go—let it die away—go on through that period of death into the quieter interest and happiness that follow—and you will find you are living in a world of new thrills all the time.
>
> But if you decide to make thrills your regular diet and try to prolong them artificially, they will all get weaker and weaker, and fewer and fewer, and you will be a bored, disillusioned old man for the rest of your life.[8]

In the letter "To a Former Pupil" of January 20, 1942 in *The Letters of C.S. Lewis*, he says,

> *No amount* of falls will really undo us if we keep on picking ourselves up each time. We shall of course be v. muddy and tattered children by the time we reach home. But the bathrooms are all ready, the towels put out, and the clean clothes in the airing cupboard.[9]

In that same book is a letter of December 22, 1942 to Sister Penelope in which he says, "I always tell people not to bother about 'feelings' in their prayers."[10] There is also the letter to Mrs. Sonia Graham of May 15, 1952 in which he says,

> Excitement, of whatever sort, never lasts. This is the push to start you off on your first bicycle: you'll be left to lots of dogged pedalling later on. And no need to feel depressed about it either.... [E]njoy it as a treat, not as something normal.[11]

The advice C.S. Lewis gave Mrs. Ray Garrett of Salt Lake City on September 12, 1960 sounds like the sort he had first given himself at the time of his conversion when he first knew what "Joy" was about, and then gave others throughout his life, in books and in letters, for it comprises some of the best and most needed advice Lewis ever gave. And, concludes Walter Hooper, "It's advice that I need new doses of all the time!"[12]

END NOTES

1 C.S. Lewis's letter is found in William Clayton Kimball; "The Christian Commitment: C.S.Lewis and the Defense of Doctrine," *BYU Studies* (X11:2, Winter 1972), p.188. The letter is reprinted here with the permission of C.S. Lewis Pte. Ltd. Although I haven't seen the original I assume the emphasis is Lewis's. I am grateful to Walter Hooper for securing permission (Hooper to Janes, February 4, 1994).

2 Stephen L. Schofield to Janes, March 10 and July 8, 1993. See *George MacDonald*, ed. C.S. Lewis (New York: Collier Books, 1986), p.xxv.

3 Sheldon Vanauken to Janes, December 12, 1992.

4 Peter Kreeft to Janes, May 3, 1995.

5 Walter Hooper to Janes, December 4, 1993. Emphasis in original.

6 C.S. Lewis, *The Pilgrim's Regress: An Allegorical Apology for Christianity, Reason and Romanticism* (Grand Rapids, MI: Eerdmans, 1958), pp. 161-162.

7 C.S. Lewis, *The Screwtape Letters* (Charlotte, NC: Commission Press, 1976), Letter #15, p.77.

8 C.S. Lewis, *Mere Christianity* (New York: Macmillan, 1960), pp.99-101.

9 *Letters* of *C.S. Lewis*, ed., with a memoir, by W.H. Lewis (San Diego, CA: Harcourt Brace Jovanovich, 1966), p. 199. Emphasis in original.

10 *Ibid.*, p.202.

11 *Ibid.*, p.241.

12 Hooper to Janes, December 4, 1993.

SHERWOOD ELIOT WIRT
INTERVIEWS C.S. LEWIS

By Burton K. Janes

In 1979, when I first put my hand to serious writing, I read a delightful little book, *Getting Into Print: Solid Help for Christian Writers* by Sherwood Eliot Wirt with Ruth McKinney (Nashville, Tennessee: Thomas Nelson Inc., 1977). I especially enjoyed the transcript of Wirt's exclusive interview with C.S. Lewis on May 7, 1963 (pp. 107-119; also printed in *Decision*, the official publication of the Billy Graham Evangelistic Association, September and October 1963; and C.S. Lewis, *God in the Dock: Essays on Theology and Ethics*, ed., Walter Hooper [Grand Rapids, Michigan: William B. Eerdmans Publishing Company, 1970]).

On that day, Wirt had driven to Cambridge, England, to interview "one of the world's most brilliant and widely read Christian authors." His *raison d'être* was "to learn from him how young men and women could be encouraged to take up the defense of the faith through the written word."

Earlier in his book, Wirt lists "guidelines for an interview." He writes about the "pitfalls to avoid in obtaining an writing a successful interview": a poor subject, inane questions, faulty equipment, deficient writing, and dull layout (pp. 96-99). "C.S. Lewis made a breakthrough and today his influence is greater than at the time of his death in 1963,"

Wirt observes. "God is looking for a younger Lewis who has a willingness to master written expression" (p. 26).

Wirt writes fondly of his encounter with Lewis:

> It was quickly evident that this interview was going to be different from any I had ever been granted. I found Mr. Lewis in a wing of the brick quadrangle at Magdalene College, Cambridge University, where he was professor of Medieval and Renaissance literature. I climbed a flight of narrow, incredibly worn, wooden steps, knocked at an ancient wooden door with the simple designation, "Prof. Lewis," and was shown in by the housekeeper.
>
> Passing through a simply furnished parlour, I came into a study that was quite Spartan in appearance. Professor Lewis was seated at a plain table upon which reposed an old-fashioned alarm clock and an old-fashioned inkwell. I was immediately warmed by his jovial smile and cordial manner as he rose to greet me; he seemed the classic, friendly, jolly Englishman. He indicated a straight-backed chair and then sat down, snug in his tweed jacket and two sweaters, and we were away. (pp. 107-108)

Lewis spoke incisively on many topics, including the following:

Writing: "Writing is like a 'lust,' or like 'scratching when you itch.' Writing comes as a result of a very strong impulse, and when it comes, I for one must get it out."

His conversion: "I was the object rather than the subject in this affair. I was decided upon. ... [W]hat I heard was God saying, 'Put down your gun and we'll talk.' "

Encountering Jesus Christ: "You can't lay down any pattern for God. There are many different ways of bringing people into His Kingdom, even some ways that I especially dislike!"

The de-Christianization of modern culture: "The gospel ... is directly opposed to the world. ... It is not easy to be a believer in the face of ... surface evidence. It calls for a strong faith in Jesus Christ."

Discipline in the Christian life: "It is always just possible that Jesus Christ meant what He said when He told us to seek the secret place and to close the door."

Space travel: "I look forward with horror to contact with the other inhabited planets, if there are such. ... Once we find ourselves spiritually awakened, we can go to outer space and take the good things with us."

Well into the interview, Wirt asked Lewis about those evangelists who ask "people to come to a point of decision regarding the Christian life." As part of Lewis's answer, he said,

> In a civilization like ours, I feel everyone has to come to terms with the claims of Jesus Christ upon his life, or else be guilty of inattention or of evading the question. In the Soviet Union it is different. Many people living in Russia today have never had to consider the claims of Christ because they have never heard of those claims.
>
> In the same way we who live in English-speaking countries have never really been forced to consider the claims, let us say, of Hinduism. But in our Western civilization we are obligated both morally and intellectually to come to grips with Jesus Christ; if we refuse to do so we are guilty of being bad philosophers and bad thinkers. (p. 117)

Wirt obviously had found an excellent subject for his interview and asked insightful questions. His equipment performed well. He transcribed the interview into crisp prose. The layout of the transcribed interview is interesting and arresting. Readers of Lewis are grateful for his clear, precise and unencumbered style captured in Wirt's interview with him.

Appendix

STEPHEN L. SCHOFIELD
(1915-93)*

By Burton K. Janes

Stephen Leonard Schofield, the founding publisher and editor of *The Canadian C.S. Lewis Journal*, was born on Tuesday, July 13, 1915, at his grandparents' home, "Oakwood," in London, Ontario, but he spent all of his young life in Montreal, Quebec. He had one sister, Marjorie (Mrs. A.G. Thompson of Montreal).

Around eight years of age, Stephen was diagnosed as being profoundly deaf, having contracted scarlet fever at five. He attended several private and state schools, one of which was Trinity College School in Port Hope, Ontario, which he thoroughly enjoyed and where he made many lifelong friends. He entered McGill University in Montreal to study engineering, but was unable to complete his studies. He later returned to McGill to study drafting, which he used in his father's firm, R and M Bearings.

Stephen tried desperately to be admitted to the Services during World War II, but was turned down. While working for his father in Vancouver, British Columbia, he was given a book by C.S. Lewis. It

---

*I am grateful to Esther Schofield for providing me with the information with which much of this article was written.

was either *The Screwtape Letters* or *Broadcast Talks*. At that time, Stephen was feeling low because all of his friends were away fighting. Although he had been brought up in church and his father had for years been a warden of Christ Church Cathedral in Montreal, church itself made little impact on the younger man until he read Lewis.

In 1942 he published and distributed 2,000 copies of the first of a series of tracts for Canadian clergy, "Towards Extending the Church's Influence—Anywhere," in which he wrote eloquently of the clergy's passion. His publication elicited a positive response from many readers, including Harry Emerson Fosdick, who thanked the author for his "very interesting monograph on the art of illustrating sermons."

Stephen decided to take up writing, wanting to work on a newspaper. In 1950 he toured England on his bicycle, gathering human interest stories. He subsequently sold articles to papers in Canada, Australia and New Zealand. In 1951 he visited Oxford and met Lewis in the Mitre Hotel, and sought out several Commonwealth students, including the film producer, Paul Almond, who became a lifelong friend. Stephen recalled later:

> In Oxford one morning I parked my bicycle against Magdalen Tower and entered the College to meet a don who had kindly invited me to lunch. He was already waiting—a rather bald man in creaseless flannels and a battered jacket. "Mr. Scho*field?*" he queried, his inflection rising with a full-flavoured Churchillian zing. I nodded; and without another word he led me to the dining room where we sat at a corner table for two. During the meal and afterwards, for about an hour, he gave me his entire attention such as I had never received from anyone. When he spoke his eyes shone; they gleamed, they were lustrous. His presence stimulated me. Such was my first impression of Lewis.

Stephen worked on various Canadian papers, as well as an American weekly. While working on *The Daily Gleaner* in Fredericton, New Brunswick, he met Esther Palin, a native of Montreal who was headmistress of Netherwood School for Girls in Rothesay. They were married in 1956. In 1960 they moved to England with two young children, Elaine and Ted. In 1962 a third child—Wood—was born.

Stephen then spent two and a half years researching his book, *Musketoon* (Jonathan Cape Limited, 1964), the riveting story of nine British, two Norwegians, and one Canadian who, in September 1942, carried out a commando raid on the large hydro-electric power station at Glomfjord in Northern Norway, which supplied power to an aluminum factory of great importance to Germany. His widow thinks he had "always felt that he had to do something to honour those who had fought, whereas he had not." It was, she recalls, amazing and exciting how he managed to locate fragments of information and slowly piece them together. He wrote hundreds of letters, enclosing self-addressed envelopes to every man in a regiment or a P.O.W. camp, seeking information. As a result, he discovered what had happened to eight out of the twelve men who had disappeared without trace: Hitler had had them shot. The dust jacket promised " a vivid and authentic narrative full of suspense and action." Published as part of the Morley War Classics series and including several photographs, the book was a crowing achievement to the author and one of which he continued to be proud.

In 1964 the Schofields bought a house in Dunsford, Godalming, Surrey, which they named "Beavers" from their Canadian backgrounds and where they lived for the next twenty-eight years. They increased their property to six acres. Stephen was keen to have ponies and a horse for their children. With a couple of dogs and a horse, he didn't need to hear! Becoming interested in riding for the disabled, he bought a horse-box so he could collect ponies and deliver them to the centre where those children were being taught. (Following Stephen's death, his family suggested donations to this cause in lieu of flowers). All of the family members rode horses in varying degrees, with Elaine being the best. Esther also had chickens and a house-cow. She thinks that despite the work involved, this was the happiest time in Stephen's life.

At the same time, Stephen was trying to publish articles and a book about Lewis. His plan was to interview people who had known Lewis, such as Kenneth Tynan, Malcolm Muggeridge, and others. His proposed book didn't materialize at that time, but he was able to use the material he had collected in his *Canadian C.S. Lewis Journal*, which masde its debut in January 1979. During those years, Clyde S. Kilby was a great friend to Stephen, and he often visited the Schofields. Many others whom Stephen had met through his *Journal*, such as Lyle W. Dorsett and the late Kathryn Lindskoog, visited the couple in Surrey. There were also many friends and relatives from Canada who visited. The Schofield home seemed always to be full.

I wondered how Stephen came to initiate another periodical devoted to Lewis. "Not much of a 'story' there," he responded. "I'd been trying for years in vain to compile/write a book about CSL; and about 1978 or 1979 I thought, *Well, if I started a journal I'd certainly have ample material for a year or so.*" His dream became a reality. By the time of his death in 1993 he had edited and published eighty-three numbers of his *Journal*, the last eleven produced under unusually trying circumstances.

Stephen finally succeeded in having a book on Lewis published. *In Search of C.S. Lewis* (Bridge Publishing, Inc., 1983), dedicated "To Esther, Elaine, Ted and Wood, with love," consists of material that originally appeared in his *Journal*. The release of the book marked another significant personal achievement. His book tackled such questions as: Why was Lewis not made a professor at Oxford? Why was it considered wrong for him to have so many readers? Why was he prejudiced against women? And against Americans? Why did he marry a dying American with two sons? "This book," he wrote, "is an attempt to shed new light on Lewis, chiefly through friends and pupils." He warned readers:

> It is not all favourable. Some Lewis enthusiasts will not like this book, at least certain parts of it. I cannot help that. As far as I can ascertain, it is all true. And surely that is what Lewis would have wanted. As one pupil says, "It would be his wish: 'Speak of me as I am; nothing extenuate, nor aught set down in malice.'" (p. xi)

As early as 1987 Stephen was methodically compiling another work tentatively entitled *Surprising Letters to "The Canadian C.S. Lewis Journal."* However, in 1988 he abandoned the idea. In the same year, he was planning to have several issues of his Journal published in book form, entitled *Lewis Marches On*. That dream failed to materialize.

Stephen was, according to his widow, a very strong believer. She suspects that he never doubted his faith during his life. He prayed regularly, and often when Esther would go to his room to ask a question he would be on his knees. Sometimes she would wonder what she had done to cause him to ask for help so often!

He possessed another characteristic. "He was also a man of rules," Esther remembers. "He would decide to do something and that would become a rule of his life, and do it he would—whatever." Nor did he care what others thought of him. One example will suffice:

> When we first moved to Dunsfold [Esther writes], he went to a conservative meeting and announced in a loud voice—he never spoke quietly—that he was going to vote Labour because the Conservatives had been in too long. Not the way to make friends in a strange place!

Nevertheless, many who were there later became the Schofields' friends when they realized Stephen's worth. He adored his family and would do anything he thought was good and right for them. Unfortunately, his deafness prevented him from listening to them and he didn't get to know them as he should have. But Esther has no doubt that the entire family benefited greatly from his strong faith. Music was a large part of Stephen. Each morning he played both the piano and clarinet (he heard the latter through his teeth). Because he was unable to sight-read, he learned pieces and played them repeatedly.

Readers of Stephen's *Journal* were saddened to read in Issue #72 that ill health might prevent him from producing anything further. He had been diagnosed with lymphoma, cancer of the lymph gland. Amazingly, he put out another eleven issues, the final one appearing in Summer 1993 (#83). In the same *Journal* he wrote:

> The anti-cancer treatment, chemotherapy, debilitates one's leg muscles, not the dexterity of one's fingers. However, my condition has of late improved considerably. Using two sticks I can walk, slowly about half a mile a day, and work at

my desk for two or three hours at a time. And today ... I revisited the hospital and doctor (after two months): he says the cancer has receded, which means I am being granted a remission: although, he said, the cancer cannot be cured in my case.

Not without significance did Stephen quote Ann Moorey's poem, "Waiting to go Home," in Issue #73. His sense of humour remained intact, as is evident from something he wrote four issues later:

Of late the autumn weather had been sunny. I was telling our housekeeper, Rosemary, that these steroid pills—which keep me alive—the doctor was changing the dose. And I said I was going to do *exactly* what he said because "I don't want to pop off just yet." "Oh, no" said Rosemary, "*not* while the weather's so nice!"

Stephen Leonard Schofield's battle with cancer ended on Thursday, August 12, 1993. On September 8, a Thanksgiving Service for his life was held at the Church of St. Mary and All Saints in Dunsfold. "The church was full with people who really cared," Esther wrote me. "They didn't come because they felt they ought."

The hymns were taken from Stephen's notebook. He had typed his favourites and learned them by heart. He would then sing them to himself on his walks. Psalm 19 was his favourite, and the Prayer of Thanksgiving was another preference. He and Esther used to say the prayer in the mornings when he would read to her and say other prayers. A friend had suggested that Lewis's "A Word About Praising" (from *Reflections on the Psalms*) be read. The Road to Emmaus episode (Luke 24:13-35) was another favourite. Esther has in her possession a tape of Pat Dixon playing Mozart's Clarinet Concerto (the slow movement).

Among the many tributes that poured into the Schofield home after Stephen's death were descriptions of the deceased as friendly, special, colourful, noble, dedicated, wonderful, ebullient, lovely, unique, courageous, generous, caring, kind, honest, forthright, bold, genuine, extraordinary, brave and great. There is no doubt that he lived life to the fullest.

Stephen commented to me, "One never knows what is around the corner!" In 1993, Roger Stronstad turned a corner and found himself as the new editor of *The Canadian C.S. Lewis Journal*. On February 1 of that year, Roger wrote Stephen for the first time, enquiring about acquiring back issues of the *Journal*. On May 18, Roger asked about buying some of Stephen's Lewisiana for the C.S. Lewis Centre which Roger was trying to establish. Stephen replied with a startling, unexpected and daunting offer:

> I am glad to offer you the right to carry on this *Journal* if you wish, presumably expanding it to [the Marion E.] Wade's writers [George MacDonald, G.K. Chesterton, C.S. Lewis, J.R.R. Tolkien, Charles Williams, Dorothy L. Sayers, and Owen Barfield]. I can send you quite a lot that may be helpful. All power to you.

He added a postscript: "I mean, of course, to carry it on, when I have died. I'm 77 and probably won't live much longer." Thus, when Stephen died on August 12 Roger found himself to be the new editor of the *Journal*.

In 2001 growing professional pressures forced Roger to make difficult decisions about the escalating busyness in his life. One decision was to cease publishing the *Journal* with Issue #100 (Autumn 2001). "This decision was not made lightly," he informed subscribers, "nor was it made without regret. But over the past couple of years it became increasingly inevitable. ... When I inherited the *Journal* following the untimely death of Stephen Schofield, I was determined to produce a product at once both informative and entertaining and which would properly honour his role as publisher of the *Journal* from 1979-93."

In 1980 the staff of *Eternity* magazine referred to *The Canadian C.S. Lewis Journal* as "a sprightly, sometimes feisty newsletter." Reflecting on the *Journal* under Stephen Schofield's editorship, I think back to a trip I made to the former Soviet Union in 1978. Back in Canada, I spent a nostalgic hour viewing Peter Ustinov's *Leningrad* on television. Later William Casselman wrote in *Maclean's* magazine, "This is the Leningrad of Peter Ustinov. Not mine, not yours perhaps, but his alone—quirky, flawed, riveting." Here is my paraphrase of Casselman:

"This is the Lewis of Stephen Schofield. Not mine, not yours perhaps, but his alone—quirky, flawed, riveting."

At the same time, these adjectives—quirky, flawed, riveting—describe the very things that sustained reader interest. Stephen's *Journal* was entertaining and informative. It was strictly the word of an avid admirer of Lewis. It was aimed at a wide audience and was controversial. It offered reprints of varying quality and lasting impact. It was not always pleasing to the eye. It accepted advertising and included photographs. It was bound to be a winner among the Lewisian aficionado. Early on, readers came to expect the unexpected, the unorthodox, the idiosyncratic. Stephen never failed to produce a lively compendium of Lewisian studies.

Kathryn Lindskoog offered an apt assessment of Stephen and his *Journal*:

> Steve Schofield's outstanding contributions to Lewis lore spanned 15 years and 83 issues—in spite of his profound hearing loss, the vicissitudes of literary controversy, and a long final illness. Steve was a true first-generation Lewis specialist—a warmly informal and spontaneous independent journalist with boundless enthusiasm and dedication.